The Thrill
of It All

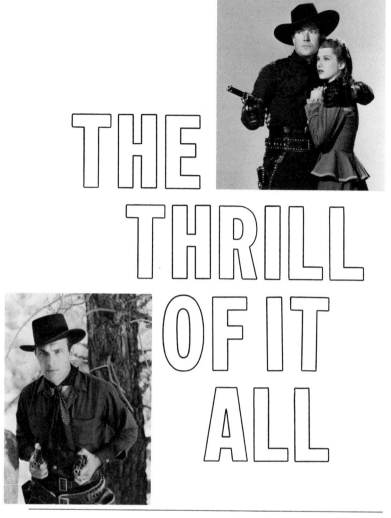

THE THRILL OF IT ALL

ALAN G. BARBOUR

COLLIER BOOKS, NEW YORK, NEW YORK

COLLIER-MACMILLAN LIMITED, LONDON

The Macmillan Company
866 Third Avenue, New York, N.Y. 10022
Collier-Macmillan Canada Ltd., Toronto, Ontario

The Thrill of It All is published in a hardcover edition by The Macmillan Company.

Library of Congress Catalog Card Number: 76-171564

First Collier Books Edition 1971

Printed in the United States of America

Dedicated to my father,
Walter Ernest Barbour,
with all the love and affection a son
can give

ACKNOWLEDGMENTS

The author wishes to express his sincere thanks and appreciation to the individuals and organizations listed below who supplied, through the years, the stills and information which have helped make this book possible.

The Individuals:
Roy Barcroft, Ernest Burns, John Cocchi, Edward Connor, Henry Kier, Ernie Kirkpatrick, Paula Klaw, Louis McMahon, Don Miller, Gray Morrow, Sloan Nibley, James Robert Parish, Marshall Reed, Mark Ricci, Stephen Sally, Jim Shoenberger, Tom Steele, Linda Stirling.

The Organizations:
Allied Artists-TV, Cinemabilia, Columbia Pictures Corp., Eagle-Lion Films, Fawcett Publications, Four Star International, Fox Film Corp., Grand National Pictures, Kier's, King Features Syndicate, Lippert Films, MCA-TV, Medallion-TV, The Memory Shop, MGM-TV, Monogram Pictures, Movie Star News, National General Corp., National Telefilm Associates, NBC-TV, Paramount-TV, Premium Products, Inc., Producers Releasing Corp., Red Ryder Enterprises, Republic Pictures Corp., RKO-Radio Pictures, Screen Gems, Inc., Screen Guild Releasing Corp., Twentieth Century-Fox, United Artists, United Artists Associated, Universal Pictures Corp., Universal-International, Warner Bros, Warner Bros-Seven Arts, Inc., William Boyd Enterprises.

With Special Thanks To:
Jean Barbour and Malcolm McPherson

I would also like to gratefully thank the following three close personal friends. First, William K. Everson, the film historian, who graciously lent me many rare stills from his private collection for use in my survey of the B-Western, and whose own best-selling book, *A Pictorial History of the Western Film* (Citadel Press), furnished invaluable background information; second, Bob Price and Sam Sherman, whose definitive articles on both great and obscure Western stars in magazines like *Wildest Westerns* and *Screen Thrills Illustrated* also provided me with much essential reference material. Almost everyone who writes or studies the Western film genre invariably "borrows," and neglects to credit, factual material from these three men, and I would like to personally take this opportunity to thank them and acknowledge their valuable and extensive contributions.

CONTENTS

PREFACE

One of the most moving and poignant moments I have ever witnessed on the motion picture screen was not in a sequence from a regular theatrical feature but rather in a short filmed prologue made with cowboy great William S. Hart in 1939 to introduce his famous silent epic Western *Tumbleweeds*, which United Artists was reissuing to theatres. In this brief foreword Hart, then in his late sixties, presented the audience with historical information about the opening up of the famed Cherokee Strip, with its famous landrush, on which *Tumbleweeds* was based. Then, in the final moments of this historic film clip, Hart, his voice tremulous and charged with emotion, his body tense with enthusiasm and fists clenched, summed up for the audience not only what he felt, but what every true lover of the B-Western has similarly felt at one time or another in his life:

"My friends, I loved the art of making motion pictures. It is as the breath of life to me. The rush of the wind as it cuts your face. The pounding hoofs of the pursuing posse. Out there in front—a fallen tree trunk that spans a yawning chasm, and an old animal under you that takes it in the same low, ground-eating gallop. The harmless shots of the baffled ones that remained behind and then . . . the clouds of dust through which comes the faint voice of the director: 'Okay, Bill, okay! Glad you made it. Great stuff, Bill, great stuff and say, Bill, give old Fritz [Hart's famous horse] a pat on the nose for me, will ya?' Oh—the thrill of it all!"

I'm with you, Bill, and give old Fritz a pat for me, too.

Alan G. Barbour
1971

The Thrill
of It All

Looking at this scene of Tom Mix sitting astride his famous horse, Tony, it is easy to see why millions of movie fans made him the most popular Western screen idol of them all.

1

SILENT
HOOFBEATS

The short happy life of the American B-Western very closely paralleled that of a man. It was born, suffered growing pains, matured, reached peaks of outstanding success and sank to valleys of utter failure, and finally grew senile and died prematurely after a lifespan of about fifty years.

The birth of the genre took place in 1903 when, after a few very short experimental films were made featuring scenes of contemporary Western action of brief fictionalized historical incidents, the Edison Company made *The Great Train Robbery*. The film ran for only about ten minutes, but within that time span it told a complete story of a robbery, with chase and final action-packed showdown. It wasn't much, but it was a beginning, and other studios made copies to cash in on the original's success. About 1908 G. M. Anderson, who had played several small parts in *The Great Train Robbery*, made a short Western called *Broncho Billy and the Baby*. It had an interesting plot line which found Anderson playing a "good" badman who sacrifices himself to save a child. The name "Broncho Billy" caught on, and Anderson made hundreds of one- and two-reel Westerns based on the character he had developed and he became the screen's very first Western hero.

The further development of the Western format was enhanced in the 1908-1913 period when pioneer directors like D. W. Griffith and Thomas H. Ince both cranked out one- and two-reelers featuring such notables of the screen as Lillian Gish and Blanche Sweet as female leads.

Unlike *The Great Train Robbery*, which was shot in the "wilds" of New Jersey, Griffith shot most of his films in and around Hollywood, which was still fairly primitive country containing large stretches of uncluttered scenery. Titles came out like *The Goddess of Sagebrush Gulch*, *The Battle of Elderbush Gulch*, and *The Last Drop of Water*. The films were full of action and, at the same time, had moments of striking visual beauty. It was another step in the maturing process.

Two men who were to make enormous contributions in the development of the genre both began their screen careers at approximately the same time, in 1914. William S. Hart had a distinguished background of theatrical experience already behind him when he began appearing in one-reelers. He caught on to the new art quickly and graduated to feature-length work in a very short time. Before long he was already turning out minor classics like *Hell's Hinges* and *The Aryan*, both made in 1916. By the twenties Hart had perfected his role of the "good" badman and went on to do films like *The Testing Block*, *Three Word Brand*, and *Wild Bill Hickok* for Paramount. He made his final film in 1925: the epic *Tumbleweeds*, which Western authority William K. Everson considers worthy of being ranked with *The Covered Wagon* and *The Iron Horse*, two of the best Western films ever made. Hart, in addition to starring in *Tumbleweeds*, also co-directed the film with King Baggott. He then retired from the screen and wrote his autobiography. Many years later, in 1939, *Tumble-weeds* was reissued and Hart made a ten-minute introduction to the film in which he told the audience some facts about the opening of the Cherokee strip, and then concluded with the moving comments mentioned in the preface.

The second man who made an important impact on the development of the Western was director John Ford. He began in films as an actor and stuntman in 1914, and by 1917 Universal had signed him to direct some two-reel Westerns which featured, among other stars, Hoot Gibson and Harry Carey. Unfortunately, almost all of these films have been lost and are unavailable to historians and scholars for study, causing a noticeable gap in the appreciation of Ford's early career. Motion picture companies were, and unfortunately continue to be, fearfully shortsighted. Early films made on nitrate stock were allowed to decompose, or were simply junked, since it was felt that there would be no future use for them after their initial screenings. Rumors persist that Universal, while filming a spectacular fire sequence for a later feature film, used literally hundreds of rare original negatives as fuel, thus forever destroying many of their silent classics. Fortunately, Ford's very first film, *Straight Shooting*, made in 1917 and starring both Carey and Gibson, is one that has survived. In 1924 Ford made his classic *The Iron Horse*, and he has remained the dean of Western directors for over fifty years.

As the Western grew in popularity and men like Hart, Carey, and Gibson prospered, it was only natural that there would be a veritable rush to bring new faces to the screen in outdoor action dramas. Men like William Desmond, Roy Stewart, Dustin Farnum, and William Farnum were box-office favorites, and a great many others have long since been completely forgotten.

The twenties approached rapidly, and the new decade would bring more than a score of new stars into the Western fold. Some, like Buck Jones, Ken Maynard, Tim McCoy, Bob Steele, and Hoot Gibson would continue to be popular for years to come, while others like Ted Wells, Fred Thomson, Jack Hoxie, Fred Humes, and Leo Maloney would either become character actors or fade into complete oblivion.

However, of all the great stars who achieved popularity in the twenties, none was greater than Tom Mix, the most popular Western star who ever appeared on the motion picture screen.

Mix had actually begun his screen career as early as 1911; he made almost a hundred one and two-reelers for Selig, which kept him busy until 1917. At that time Fox Studios offered him a contract, and he went to work for them, appearing in such features as *Fame and Fortune, Treat 'Em Rough, Ace High, Rough Riding Romance, Fighting for Gold,* and *Western Blood.*

Between 1920 and 1928 Mix made more than sixty films, all of which helped Fox Studios pay the rent and made Mix a living idol to millions of fans, not only in the United States but around the world. In 1928 he left Fox and signed with FBO to make a brief series. When sound came in in 1929, Mix was one of those stars who couldn't make the transition, and after a brief series for Universal and a serial for Mascot he was washed up in films. His final years were spent touring with his own Tom Mix Circus, and on October 12, 1940 he was killed in an automobile accident in Arizona.

In retrospect it is easy to see why Mix had been so popular with the public. Prior to his screen career he had led an adventure-filled real life that many wished they could emulate. He fought in the Spanish-American War, was a performer in a Wild West show, was a real deputy U.S. Marshal in Oklahoma, and broke horses for the British for the Boer campaign in Africa. When he started making his films, he wanted to be completely opposite in character from William S. Hart. Where Hart stressed character studies and plodding but effective dramatic sequences, Mix wanted to feature action and more action. His films were full of chases filmed at breakneck speed and fight sequences that were models other studios worked from. He also had a tremendous flair for showmanship, and he wore the fancy clothes and frills of a type which was to become famous when worn by Autry, Rogers, and others in years to come. Even his horse, Tony, became a celebrity, often getting fan mail all his own. Small wonder a generation of film fans adored Tom Mix.

The twenties offered more new faces to Western fans than any other decade. In addition to the ones already mentioned there was Wally Wales, who later became a staple in the Western stock company of villains in sound films using the name Hal Taliaferro; Edmund Cobb, who did similar duty; Art Acord, who made many popular serials and features for Universal; Buddy Roosevelt; Buffalo Bill, Jr., whose real name was J. C. Wilsey; Bob Custer; Bill Cody;

Lane Chandler; Jack Perrin; and Jack Luden. Many future stars of greater magnitude had humble beginnings in this period. Gary Cooper made appearances in Paramount features like *Arizona Bound* and *Nevada*. William Boyd, who was to appear in classic Paramount films directed by men like Cecil B. DeMille, made his Western debut in 1926 in Pathé's *The Last Frontier*. Warner Baxter turned up in *Drums of the Desert*, a 1927 Paramount release, and Jack Holt made a long series of exciting adventures for the same studio, many of which were based on Zane Grey stories like *The Mysterious Rider*.

However, even though the decade produced a quantity of new stars, by the beginning of the sound era the genre had lost a considerable amount of general appeal, much the same way as serials lost favor at the same time. It was left to a new breed of heroes to bring fresh excitement to the Saturday afternoon oaters in the early thirties; and very few were able to do just that.

It should also be noted that many of the films made by the stars discussed above should certainly not be classified in the same B-Western category with a typical Johnny Mack Brown or Charles Starrett Western of the thirties or forties. Many of the films of Hart, Carey, Gibson, and Mix had very strong production values, and a good deal of time and money was spent to give them a quality far removed from what is normally considered a B-Western film. Out of necessity these people are grouped together to give some indication of the roots from which the little hour-long action features sprang.

Bob Kortman, with cigar, and Broncho Billy Anderson in *The Golden Trail*, one of the hundreds of two-reel Westerns the first cowboy hero of the screen turned out.

Don Coleman achieved a small degree of success in films like *The Bronc Stomper* (Pathé 1928).

A portrait of G. M. "Broncho Billy" Anderson.

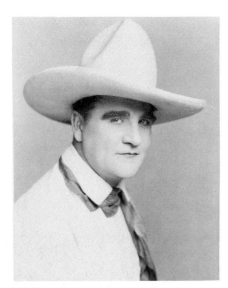

William S. Hart in his classic epic Western, *Tumbleweeds* (United Artists 1925).

William Desmond was a big favorite of silent film audiences, and went on to do excellent character roles in talking features.

4

Jesse J. Goldburg
presents

BILL CODY in
'Westerns That
Are Different'

Bill Cody met with some degree of fame in silent
Westerns, but lost out when sound came in. This
is a general advertising poster put out to promote
Bill.

Few people can recall Jack Padjan, *left*, but most
film lovers fondly recall his opponent in this scene
from *Crashing Through* (Pathé 1928): Tom San-
tschi made hundreds of films, including *The
Spoilers* in which he had a classic battle with William Farnum.

Harry Carey, a major star of silent Westerns and in later years one of the screen's most beloved character actors.

Would you like to bet whether or not Leo Maloney will really make that obviously staged leap in this scene from *Border Blackbirds* (Pathé 1927)?

Fred Kohler, *center*, has obvious plans for Sally Blane, but Jack Luden has other thoughts in mind in *Shootin' Irons* (Paramount 1927).

Jack Hoxie and Elinor Field in *Don Quickshot of The Rio Grande* (Universal 1923).

Billy Franey and Bill Cody in *King of the Saddle* (Associated Exhibitors 1926).

Fred Thomson, here seen in *The Pioneer Scout* (Paramount 1928), was one of the few stars who was able to give Tom Mix any real competition at all.

Jack Holt parlayed his pleasing personality and athletic ability into an outstanding early film career. This portrait is from *Man of the Forest* (Paramount 1926).

Jack Holt is behind that serape in *The Mysterious Rider* (Paramount 1927), one of numerous films based on stories by Zane Grey.

Buddy Roosevelt, *left*, and Robert Homans, *right*, get the goods on Lafe McKee in
The Bandit Buster (Pathé 1927).

Harry Woods gets the drop on a furry-clad Buck Jones while Eva Novak gives him a
gentle hint in *30 Below Zero* (Fox 1926).

Tom Mix and a fuzzy scene-stealer in *Fighting for Gold* (Fox 1919).

Famous silent hero Tom Mix in a pensive scene from *Do and Dare* (Fox 1922).

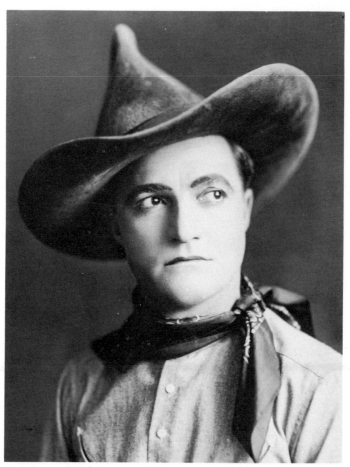

Tom Mix, the most popular of all the great Western heroes of the screen.

11

Buck Jones delivers his brand of justice to Fred Kohler in *Outlawed Guns* (Universal 1935). Notice Fred's deformed right hand, which he usually concealed from the camera's eye or explained away by saying that some gunman had shot off his fingers.

2
BEST OF
THE BREED

As the third decade of the twentieth century began, the great Western heroes of the silent screen found themselves facing a villain more deadly than any they had opposed on the screen to date: sound! The movies could now speak to their audiences and, unfortunately, a large majority of silent saddleburners sounded simply terrible and found their careers wiped out almost overnight. The mightiest to fall was Tom Mix, who as a silent star had achieved unbelievable popularity with Western fans. He made one series of talkies for Universal that had some good action sequences, and a serial for Mascot, *The Miracle Rider*, which was his last starring film; then he rode off into the second-class world of rodeo, circus, and fair appearances as a once-great movie idol. But there were several stars, six to be exact, who did adapt well to the new sound medium and who became the giant stars of the early thirties: Buck Jones, Tim McCoy, Hoot Gibson, Tom Tyler, Ken Maynard, and Bob Steele.

Buck Jones, whose real name was Charles Gebhart, had had a wide variety of jobs before breaking into films around 1917; he had worked on a ranch as a cowpuncher, worked as a mechanic at the famous Indianapolis racetrack, done army service in the Philippines and trick riding with a wild West show and, eventually, made appearances with the famous Ringling Bros Circus. He entered films by appearing in bit roles in two-reelers and features and as a stuntman extraordinaire. Fox Studios finally gave him his big break in 1920 by starring him in *The Last Straw*. After that he appeared in dozens of features for the studio throughout the twenties. Around 1928 he tried to go into independent production, but failed badly with a film called *The Big Hop*. Another big failure was the Buck Jones Wild West Show, which he put together in 1929. He made his first talkie, *The Lone Rider*, for Columbia in 1930. After a string of further adventures for that studio, he made a series under his own production banner and released them through Universal from 1934 to 1937. On occasion Buck would venture from the Western range to do straight dramas, but those films were generally met with token approval. Jones continued making films and serials, with some lessening of his popularity, right through to 1942, when he was killed in the tragic Coconut Grove fire in Boston.

Hoot Gibson also had real-life experience as a working cowboy before he entered silent pictures as a player and stuntman. He got his first chance to shine in a series of two-reelers produced by Universal in 1919. A year later he made *Action*, his first full-length film under the direction of John Ford. After that film he made a long series of starring films for Universal, and became one of the studio's biggest box-office draws. Unlike most of the cowboy stars, Hoot tried to inject humor into his roles. He was always throwing in wisecracks or clowning around. He seldom wore a regular gun and holster, but rather carried his six-shooter either in his boot or in his belt. Hoot found the going a little rough when sound came in. He made a series in 1931–1932, had a few scattered roles in 1935 (including an excellent part in the all-star Three Mesquiteers film made by RKO, *Powdersmoke Range*), and made another series in 1936. In 1937 he made an appearance in the Republic serial *The Painted Stallion,* but he really had little to do. After that he was to remain off the screen until the early forties, when he popped up again in the Trail Blazers series for Monogram, which was met with mixed feelings.

Tom Tyler, who had changed his name from Vincent Markowski for screen use, wanted to be a performer from his earliest days. He finally worked his way to Hollywood and entered the film industry as a prop man and stunt double. His first Western features were made in 1925, and he continued making outdoor thrillers for FBO Studios until 1928. The following year he made another series for Syndicate Pictures with titles like *The Man from Nevada, The Canyon of Missing Men,* and *Call of the Desert.* His first talking starrer was the serial *Phantom of the West,* made in ten chapters by Mascot. It wasn't a very good film, but Tom came across well, and in 1931 he made his first sound feature Western, *West of Cheyenne.* Throughout the remainder of the thirties he was to do Westerns and serials for Universal, Monogram, Syndicate, and other studios in an apparently endless stream as his popularity continued. In the forties he gained fame as one of the Three Mesquiteers, as the hero of two serials, *Adventures of Captain Marvel* and *The Phantom,* and as a fine character actor in numerous big-budget features. When his health began to deteriorate in the late forties, Tom spent his remaining years doing bit and small featured roles, usually as a villain, for assorted studios. It was a sad finish to a relatively illustrious screen career.

Ken Maynard was a much better rider than actor (and there are those who maintain that his brother was an even greater rider and actor) in a long screen career that began in 1924. Ken, like Buck Jones, had also been featured with the Ringling Bros circus when he was discovered by director Lynn Reynolds and urged to make a screen test. He was successful in the test, and was signed to do a series that included such films as *The Demon Rider, The Grey Vulture,* and *Fighting Courage* for independent producer Charles Davis. Ken was signed by First National and made more than fifteen productions for the studio between 1926 and 1929. In later years, when John Wayne became a star in a short series for Warner Bros, stock footage from many of these early Maynard films was utilized quite extensively. Ken then did a brief series for Universal which was released in silent versions and in a synchronized sound system (done with recordings) that featured mostly music and sound effects. His first real talkies appeared in 1930 when he did a series for Tiffany (*Alias the Bad Man, Pocatello Kid, Hellfire Austin,* and others) which lasted until 1932. Bouncing from studio to studio, Ken made features for World-Wide, Universal, Mascot, and Columbia. Like Hoot Gibson, Ken made a screen comeback in the Monogram Trail Blazers series in six productions and then, after appearing in an Astor-released feature called *Harmony Trail,* retired from the screen. Maynard, who once was one of the biggest Western stars ever, spent all his money and now lives in the humblest of circumstances in a run-down trailer camp in the San Fernando valley.

Tim McCoy was one of the most likable performers of all the great Western stars of the period. An acknowledged authority on Indian folklore, Colonel Tim began his screen career in the MGM production of *War Paint* in 1926, after having served as a technical advisor on such film classics as *The Covered Wagon* and *The Vanishing American.* His MGM films were all well-done little gems filled with good location work, often made on authentic Indian Reservations, and good action sequences. Tim made his entrance into talkies by appearing in the first talking serial, Universal's *The Indians Are Coming.* He did another serial for the same studio a year later, *Heroes of the Flames,* and then moved over to Columbia where he made sixteen films in two years, among them *Texas Cyclone, Rusty Rides Alone, The Western Code,* and *The Riding Tornado.* The following year Columbia put Tim into a series of non-Western features, but McCoy, though he turned in excellent performances, was not cut out to do things like *Police Car 17, Hold the Press,* and *Speed Wings,* and the next year he was back in the saddle for another series of Westerns for the studio. McCoy, following in the footsteps of all the other stars of the time, then bounced from studio to studio doing work for Puritan, Victory, Monogram and, in the forties, PRC. In 1941–1942 Tim joined Buck Jones and Raymond Hat-

14

Ken Maynard and his horse, Tarzan, in a scene from *Fighting Through* (Tiffany 1930).

ton in Monogram's popular Rough Riders films and then called it quits. He did appear on television with his own show in which he demonstrated his Indian knowledge, and he made brief appearances in films like *Around the World in 80 Days* and *Run of the Arrow* in the fifties, and in Alex Gordon's *Requiem for a Gunfighter* in the sixties he looked a great deal better than the film's much-younger star, Rod Cameron. He now spends his time touring with circus shows.

Rounding out this action sextet was young Bob Steele. Born Robert Bradbury, Jr., he and his twin brother, Bill, broke into films at an extremely early age when their famous director-father photographed them, originally for fun only, in film which was eventually released as a series of two-reelers in the mid-twenties under the overall title of *Adventures of Bill and Bob*. In 1927 Steele made his first starring Western, *The Mojave Kid*, and followed that with thirteen more titles which were all released by FBO. These were followed by seven films made for Syndicate Pictures in 1929–1930. His first talkie was *Near the Rainbow's End*, made in 1930, and was followed by thirteen more titles in 1931–1932. The following year he made another eight features, including *Gallant Fool* and *Trailing North,* and a thrilling serial for Mascot, *Mystery Squadron,* in which he and his pal

Guinn "Big Boy" Williams tracked down the mysterious Black Ace. Following the same pattern as had the other stars, Steele then bounced around doing films for Supreme, Republic, RKO (the famous *Powdersmoke Range* film mentioned earlier), Metropolitan, and, in the forties, PRC and Monogram. In among all these starring Westerns Steele had some fine character roles in features like *Of Mice and Men* and *The Big Sleep,* in which he demonstrated his acting versatility. Even recently, on television, he turned in an extraordinarily touching performance as the star of one of the *Family Affair* television shows, in which he played an old-time star who payed a visit to Brian Keith's on-screen kids who had watched his old films on TV (they actually used some of Bob's old footage); the children were disappointed to find their cowboy idol an elderly has-been, but were eventually won over by his charm and personality. It was an excellent showcase appearance for a fine performer.

It is, of course, hard to capsulize six full-length careers spanning literally hundreds of screen appearances in only a few brief paragraphs, but these men really need no written words to describe their invaluable contributions to Western screen history. Their films speak for them.

Come out from behind that mask, Buck Jones. We
know it's you in *Sunset of Power* (Universal 1936).

Lona Andre was Buck Jones's leading lady in his Northwest Mounted Police adventure
Border Brigands (Universal 1935).

Helen Mack and Buck Jones in *California Trail* (Columbia 1933).

Ward Bond, *left*, and Bob Kortman are about to receive a slight surprise from Buck Jones in *The Crimson Trail* (Universal 1935).

LeRoy Mason looks like he's getting the worst of things from Buck Jones in *When a Man Sees Red* (Universal 1934).

June Gale gives Hoot Gibson a knowing look in *Rainbow's End* (First Division 1935).

Hoot Gibson connects with Roger Williams while Lafe McKee watches in this scene from *Frontier Justice* (First Division 1936).

Rex Lease, in black, gives Hoot Gibson a good wrapping up in *Cavalcade of the West* (Diversion 1936).

Lafe McKee, Hal Taliaferro, Hoot Gibson, and Bob Kortman in one of Hoot's best talking films, *Swifty* (First Division 1936).

In this scene from *Partners of the Trail* (Monogram 1931) Tom Tyler, *right*, gives Reginald Sheffield a helping hand. Sheffield was the father of young Johnny Sheffield, who became Boy in the Tarzan films.

I think Tom Tyler wants Slim Whittaker to keep
his mouth shut in *The Man from New Mexico*
(Monogram 1932).

Bob Kortman, *left*, seems to be encouraging Al
Bridge, in the buckskin outfit, to fight with Tom
Tyler, *center*, while others try to keep them apart
in *The Forty-Niners* (Freuler Films 1932).

Ken Maynard makes one of his more subtle entrances in *Gun Justice* (Universal 1934).

Ken Maynard tries his fist on Fred Kohler's jaw for size in *The Fiddlin' Buckaroo* (Universal 1933).

Ken Maynard gets the drop on Bob Kortman, Lucile Browne, and plane in *King of the Arena* (Universal 1933).

Ken Maynard does some fiddlin' and foolin' with Charles King, *right*, and Frank
Yaconelli in *Strawberry Roan* (Universal 1933).

That's Rex Lease lying on the ground after Tim McCoy has taken care of him in *Code of the Rangers* (Monogram 1938).

Charles King, *right*, and Karl Hackett are about to meet Tim McCoy face to face in *Phantom Ranger* (Monogram 1938).

A general ad mat for Tim McCoy's films; different titles would be placed under his name.

A nice portrait of Tim from his Columbia days of the early thirties.

A picturesque shot of Tim McCoy in *Phantom Ranger* (Monogram 1938).

Marion Shilling and Joe Sawyer get a glassy stare from Tim McCoy in *The Westerner* (Columbia 1935).

Harry Strang, Lane Chandler, Tim McCoy, John Merton, and Betty Compson in *Two Gun Justice* (Monogram 1938). Tim frequently used the gimmick of dressing up like a Mexican and using a dialect which didn't always sound totally convincing.

I wonder if Tim McCoy, *right*, is trying to teach Lafe McKee some of his Indian folk-lore in this scene from *End of the Trail* (Columbia 1933).

A mustache-less Charles King, *left*, gets an unhelping hand from young Bob Steele in *The Fighting Champ* (Monogram 1932).

George Hayes and Bob Steele discover something important in *Breed of the Border* (Monogram 1933), directed by Bob's father, Robert Bradbury, Sr.

A nice portrait of Bob Steele from *The Ridin' Fool* (Tiffany 1931).

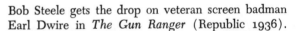

Bob Steele gets the drop on veteran screen badman Earl Dwire in *The Gun Ranger* (Republic 1936).

Bob Steele has bested Charles King again, to the obvious approval of Earl Dwire, *left*, in *The Trusted Outlaw* (Republic 1937).

Doris Hill and George Hayes shared billing with Bob Steele in *Trailing North* (Monogram 1933).

A favorite portrait of John "Duke" Wayne from the thirties.

3

SINGIN' SANDY MAKES HIS MARK

John Wayne as a *singing* cowboy? Hard as that may be for latter-day Wayne fans to believe, Duke actually did play a songbird of the saddle in several of his starring films of the thirties. Admittedly, he only mouthed the words while pros like Smith Ballew supplied the real vocals, but for the official record he did predate on the screen the eventual number-one sagebrush thrush, Gene Autry. It's a dubious distinction to be sure, but playing a singing cowboy was only one of a large assortment of screen characterizations Wayne was called upon to portray in that first decade of his remarkable screen career.

John Wayne, né Marion Michael Morrison, was an all-American football player for the University of Southern California when he was first noticed by the distinguished director John Ford, who was making a football film on location. Ford didn't make use of the young man at the time, but eventually the two entered into a personal and screen friendship which endures to this day, more than forty years later. Wayne actually credits Tom Mix with getting him a part-time job at Fox, where he wound up as a general prop man. One day, while he was doing a routine job for the John Ford film *Mother Machree,* the noted director singled him out and gave him an unbilled bit part in the film. It was the beginning of the long climb to the peak of screen stardom.

Wayne did a series of bit roles in between 1928 and 1930 before Ford encouraged fellow-

director Raoul Walsh to give the young man the lead role in his ambitious production of *The Big Trail.* Walsh heeded the suggestion, had young Marion Morrison officially change his name to John Wayne, and hoped a new star would be born. Unfortunately, it didn't quite work out that way. *The Big Trail* was, on most counts, a true epic Western filled with wonderfully cinematic tableaus filmed in picturesque locations, and pictorially the film still holds up well today; but in acting talent it is sadly lacking. Wayne simply wasn't yet ready for the big push upward. He was young, inexperienced, and awkward, and his delivery of lines was far from satisfactory. Matched up against such notable hams as Tyrone Power, Sr., and Ian Keith, his deficiencies became even more apparent. However, on the plus side was the fact that he did photograph well, and he was able to be convincing in the action sequences. At a time when sound pictures were just beginning to make themselves felt, Wayne certainly should have made enough impression to launch himself in a more than routine way, but the higher-ups at Fox failed to capitalize on the young star's potential. They threw him into a couple of straight dramas as a follow-up to *The Big Trail,* and both Wayne and the studio were disappointed.

Wayne left Fox and went over to Columbia, where he played lesser roles in routine features, including an appearance with Buck Jones in *Range Feud.* In 1932 and 1933 he was bouncing around like a ball, doing screen duty at several studios. At Mascot he appeared in three full-length serials in which he received star billing, *Shadow of the Eagle, Hurricane Express,* and *The Three Musketeers.* All three films were full of the thrilling kind of action sequences that Wayne was to thrive on for most of his career. He also had top billing in a short series of B-Westerns for Warner Bros. Containing mostly stock footage from silent Ken Maynard vehicles, Wayne really had little to do in *Haunted Gold, Ride Him, Cowboy, The Big Stampede, The Telegraph Trail, Somewhere in Sonora,* and *The Man From Monterey* except fill in the gaps joining the older action sequences together. Sandwiched in among these starring roles were additional lower-billed appearances in items like *Central Airport* and *The Life of Jimmy Dolan.*

In the latter part of 1933 Wayne signed up to do a long series of starring B-Westerns produced by Lone Star Productions and released through Monogram Pictures. It was a field day for the young leading man as he rode, fought, laughed and "sang" his way through sixteen adventures with titles like *Riders of Destiny* (the first in the series and the one in which he played Singin' Sandy), *Sagebrush Trail, Blue Steel, Randy Rides Alone, The Star Packer, Rainbow Valley,* and the last in the sequence, *Paradise Canyon.* These films offered viewers more than just a pleasing new leading man. Supporting Wayne was a superb collection of fine character actors who were to form a kind of Western stock company. Heading the list was George Hayes, who alternated between playing good guys, old timers, and scheming villains. He hadn't yet tacked on the "Gabby" nickname, and often was completely cleanshaven. Appearing in almost three-quarters of the titles was stunt ace Yakima Canutt. Although on a rare occasion he might play a sympathetic role (such as Yak, the Indian in *The Star Packer*), he was usually cast as Wayne's chief antagonist. A warm relationship had sprung up between the two men when they had appeared together in earlier vehicles at Warner Bros, and Canutt was to teach Wayne most of the intricate tricks of stunt work. Credit is usually given these two men for developing the polished kind of on-screen fight which is used today. Where formerly fisticuffs were simply wildly swinging affairs with opponents lashing out at each other helter-skelter, now we had those glorious long follow-through right and left crosses and uppercuts. Though many may argue that the earlier

free-for-alls engaged in by stars like Bob Steele and Ken Maynard were more realistic, on screen they usually looked chaotic and generally awful. Other important members of the company were Earl Dwire (like Canutt, he alternated between playing good guys and bad guys), Lafe McKee, George Cleveland and Buffalo Bill, Jr. (Jay Wilsey). It should also be noted that eleven of the films were directed, and many of them written, by Robert N. Bradbury, who was cowboy star Bob Steele's real-life father.

In 1935 Monogram, Mascot, and Consolidated merged to form the new Republic Pictures Corporation. Having hit a small size bonanza with the Gene Autry features, the new company decided to give Wayne a little bigger boost up the ladder of success and spend a little more time, money, and effort on a new series of features. *Westward Ho, New Frontier, Lawless Range, The Lawless Nineties, King of the Pecos, The Oregon Trail, Winds of the Wasteland,* and *The Lonely Trail* were the result. On the whole, all eight films were topnotch Republic productions, and Wayne was maturing enormously as an actor, rapidly becoming a big box-office favorite with Western fans. But Wayne's wanderlust struck again, and he left the increasingly lucrative wide-open spaces of the Republic back lot for the uninteresting sound stages of Universal Pictures, where he starred in a series of six entertaining, non-Western programmers: *Sea Spoilers* was a Coast Guard adventure; *Conflict,* an involved prizefight yarn; *California Straight Ahead,* a race between trucks and a train; *I Cover the War,* a story of newsreel cameramen; *Idol of the Crowds,* a tale about an ice-hockey player; *Adventure's End,* in which Wayne was a pearl diver involved in a ship mutiny.

From Universal Wayne made a very brief journey to Paramount to co-star with Johnny Mack Brown in one of that studio's short (fifty-nine minutes) Zane Grey features. *Born to the West,* often reissued under the title *Hell Town,* was an entertaining feature, but really only noteworthy for the pairing of the two big-name Western heroes.

One of the most popular series of Westerns ever turned out was the long string of adventures starring the fictional Three Mesquiteers. Ray Corrigan, Robert Livingston, and Max Terhune had come together to form a magic combination that spelled box-office success in sixteen titles produced between 1936 and 1938. When they had finished the second series of

34

Wayne should have become a major star after his appearance in *The Big Trail* (Fox 1930), but he was still too inexperienced. That's Ian Keith and Marguerite Churchill with Wayne in this scene from the film.

eight films (almost all of Republic's film series with its Western stars were scheduled for eight titles per year, with very few exceptions), the studio decided to remove Livingston from the trio and feature him in some of the studio's regular dramatic features. The void left in the group had to be quickly filled, and Wayne was sought out and signed. Generally unhappy with the Universal features, Duke was only too glad to return to the Republic action plant to do one new series of eight films playing the role of Stony Brooke. Beginning with *Pals of the Saddle* in late 1938, he starred in *Overland Stage Raiders* (a thrill-packed tale which involved the hijacking of a plane carrying a valuable gold shipment), *Santa Fe Stampede, Red River Range, The Night Riders, Three Texas Steers, Wyoming Outlaw*, and a remake of the earlier *New Frontier*. By the time this series was filmed Republic had begun to master its filming techniques, and all of the slickness and polish that was to make Republic famous was very much in evidence. After these films were finished, both Wayne and Corrigan were to leave Republic, but for entirely different reasons. Corrigan, tired of second billing and wanting more money (although he was making plenty from the use of his ranch by virtually all the studios) decided to go into production for himself and,

moving to Monogram, formed the Range Busters with John "Dusty" King and his Three Mesquiteer pal, Max "Alibi" Terhune. In its own way the new trio also achieved some success, but it really couldn't compare with its earlier Republic counterpart.

For Wayne real stardom was just a few features ahead. While he was busily churning out the Mesquiteer tales, his friend John Ford was getting ready to film *Stagecoach*. The pivotal role in the basically talky drama was the Ringo Kid, a role Ford wanted only one man to play, John Wayne. A caption on one of the publicity stills of Duke for the picture proudly announced that Wayne had received the "big break" of 1938 by being chosen for the role. That was one piece of advertising copy historic for its understatement, and something rare in the annals of generally exaggerated promotional baloney.

The die was now cast. John Wayne, who wasn't quite ready for stardom when it was first offered him more than eight years earlier, would now find the going a great deal easier. Marlene Dietrich had a classic line to deliver to Wayne in *The Spoilers* a few years later: "Anything you win, you can collect." Big Duke Wayne fought ten years and earned the right to enjoy his next thirty as one of the giants in the industry.

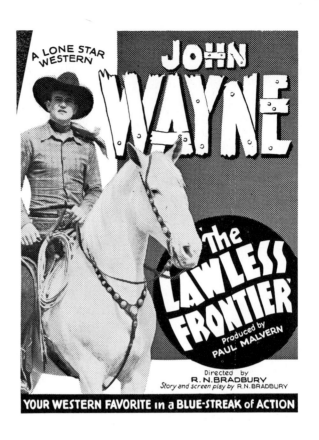

Wayne gets the drop on none other than Buck Jones in *Range Feud* (Columbia 1931).

Wayne with Sheila Terry in *Haunted Gold* (Warner
Bros 1932).

A little clowning from Luis Alberni seems to amuse Wayne in *The Man from Monterey* (Warner Bros 1933).

Wayne, Frank Rice, and Billy Franey spot something interesting in *Somewhere in Sonora* (Warner Bros 1933).

Albert J. Smith gives the Duke a little harassment of sorts in *The Telegraph Trail* (Warner Bros 1933).

Wayne in *Sagebrush Trail* (Monogram 1933), the
second of his Lone Star Westerns.

George Hayes, *center*, without his "Gabby" tag,
was the villain, along with henchman-stunt ace
Yakima Canutt, *right*, in *Randy Rides Alone*
(Monogram 1934).

Another excellent publicity photo of Wayne in the
thirties.

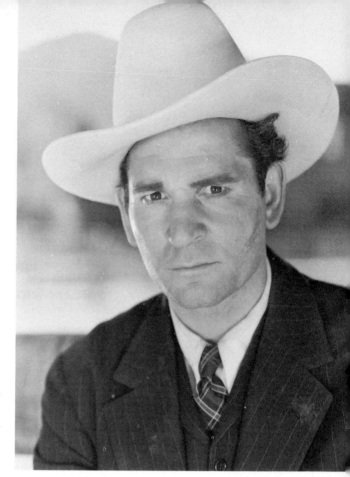

Yakima Canutt, the acknowledged dean of stunt-men, starred in many of Wayne's Lone Star films. In this portrait he is made up for his role in *Paradise Canyon* (Monogram 1935).

In another scene from *Randy Rides Alone* (Monogram 1934), Wayne and Canutt engage in one of their frequent screen battles.

Wayne has just finished giving Edward Parker a lesson in *The Star Packer* (Monogram 1934). In the background, Yakima Canutt, playing a good Indian role, takes care of Earl Dwire.

Director Robert N. Bradbury, the father of star Bob Steele, gives some directions to the cast of *Blue Steel* (Monogram 1934). Wayne is over against the rail, and in the crowd you can spot Eleanor Hunt, Ed Peil, and, right behind Peil, Yakima Canutt.

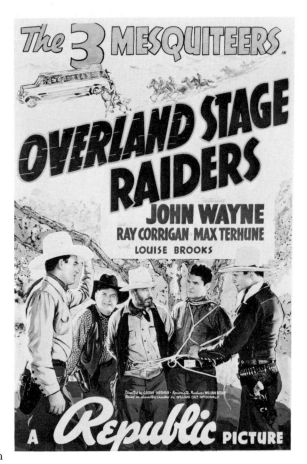

Duke Wayne gets the drop on Yakima Canutt in order to rescue Marion Burns and Earl Hodgins in *Paradise Canyon* (Monogram 1935).

John Wayne and Johnny Mack Brown teamed up in *Born to the West* (Paramount 1938), which has been retitled as *Hell Town*.

Wayne, Ray Corrigan, and Max Terhune, the Three Mesquiteers, give Dick Alexander an unexpected bath in *Santa Fe Stampede* (Republic 1938).

4
NEW TRAILS TO ADVENTURE

The thirties was a vintage decade for the new breed of Western screen hero who could adapt himself well to the sound era. Films were now beginning to require professional-caliber acting from its cowboy heroes, and those who couldn't measure up soon lost favor with audiences. The "realistic" cowboy gave way rapidly to the polished pro who could deliver dialogue with a flair, and one by one the greats of the silent era were pushed aside. Tom Mix, who was perhaps the most popular of all Western stars during his heyday of the twenties, just couldn't make the grade; after a few routine Universal efforts and a wishy-washy serial for Mascot, *The Miracle Rider,* he gave up. A new decade of Saturday afternoon matinee worshippers found its own bigger-than-life idols.

William Boyd had been a major star at Paramount during the silent film period, but he found his career turning downward rapidly in the early thirties when he appeared in a load of potboilers for studios like RKO. However, his career took a new and prosperous turn in 1935 when he made *Hop-a-Long Cassidy* for Paramount (later retitled *Hopalong Cassidy Enters*). His portrayal won instant approval from audiences and launched Boyd on a series that was to span thirteen years and produce sixty-six titles. Boyd's distinct screen personality was one of the most pleasing ever presented to viewers, and a single flash of his smile and a quick burst of his hearty laughter alone were worth the price of admission to one of his films. Throughout the series he had

the able assistance of capable partners like James Ellison, Russell Hayden, Jay Kirby, Rand Brooks, and others; he rounded out his action trio with comical sidekicks like George Hayes, who was called "Windy" a few years before he got permanently saddled with his "Gabby" nickname, and Andy Clyde as "California Carlson," as well as a few less notable players. The Cassidy films were usually filmed on location in more picturesque areas than the minor studios used, primarily because a good deal more money and time were spent on their production; they had well-written scripts and relatively long running times. During the final year of production the titles of the Cassidy films really shook up some fans who were used to things like *In Old Mexico, Hills of Old Wyoming,* and *Hidden Gold* and suddenly found titles like *The Dead Don't Dream, Sinister Journey,* and *False Paradise* flashing on their screens. Boyd later became a millionaire when he wisely bought up all the rights to his films and then put them on television.

George O'Brien was another big star in silent films, appearing in such classics as *The Iron Horse* and *Sunrise* as well as a long string of excellent Fox films based on stories by Zane Grey. O'Brien had a winning personality not unlike Boyd's, and was at his very best when he was flipping wisecracks to the assorted tough guys in his films. Extremely well-built, George often posed for professional pictures in muscle and body-building magazines and often had the

47

An important ingredient of the Hopalong Cassidy features was the use of picturesque locations like this one in which Russell Hayden, George "Gabby" Hayes, and William Boyd shot *Rustler's Valley* (Paramount 1937).

girls in the audience groaning in appreciation when he bared his expansive chest. Still in superb shape today, George can look back to his fine performances in films like *O'Malley of the Mounted, The Border Patrolman, When a Man's a Man,* and dozens of other excellent screen favorites.

When Gene Autry had made his successful appearance at Republic as a singing cowboy, it was only natural that other studios, expressing their usual lack of creative imagination, would try to cash in on the craze by bringing out some new stars as competitors. Grand National introduced popular Tex Ritter to the screen in *Song of the Gringo* in 1936, and he went on to do work at Monogram, Columbia, Universal, and PRC, appearing either solo or with such popular favorites as Johnny Mack Brown and William Elliott. Monogram also had Jack Randall, the brother of cowboy star Robert Livingston, who sang, wisely but not too well, and fought his way through a number of generally excellent productions into the forties. Randall might have become an even bigger star if he had not succumbed to a heart attack while making a Columbia serial, *The Royal Mounted Rides Again.* Even the prestigious Warner Bros tried to get their share of the matinee dollar by starring Dick Foran in a series in which he was billed as "The Singing Cowboy." Foran was a fine actor and had one of the nicer singing voices, but the series was a short one and he went on to do better work in serials and features as a star and leading character actor. Future Western star William Elliott popped up in the Foran films as a *villain.* At Universal Bob Baker was given quite a build-up as a singing hero, but his career was of short duration. Even pairing him up with Johnny Mack Brown failed to generate much real interest, although he was a pleasant and capable performer. Fred Scott had done a considerable amount of screen work in the early thirties before he turned to the saddle in 1936 to star in *Romance Rides the Range.* As "The Silvery Voiced Buckaroo," Scott appeared in titles like *Moonlight on the Range, Knight of the Plains,* and *Songs and Bullets.* It was in a Scott film called *Melody of the Plains* that comic sidekick Al St. John first acquired the "Fuzzy" nickname he was to be stuck with for the rest of his life. Ray Whitley gained his reputation as a singing sidekick to stars like Tim Holt, but he was talented enough in his own right to do a series of two-reel musical Westerns for RKO. Smith Ballew had a good voice but a very short career, and men like Art Jarret and Tex Fletcher were eliminated from the running almost immediately. The field was really cornered by Autry and, eventually, Roy Rogers over at Republic.

Though Western songbirds of quality were in relative short supply, action fans did have numerous new star favorites to rout for. Tom Keene, also called George Duryea and Richard Powers in films, had a long string of successful films made for various studios. Quick with a quip, like Boyd and O'Brien, he gave a striking image on screen in films like *The Law Commands, Rebellion, Glory Trail,* and others. Rex Bell made over a dozen Westerns in which his youthful, boyish appearance stood him in good stead, but he never really quite caught on. Although he wasn't the big screen hero he would have liked to have been, he did have the consolation prize of being married to silent screen great Clara Bow and eventually becoming Lieutenant Governor of Nevada. Kermit Maynard, Ken's younger brother, made numerous films in which he capably demonstrated his prowess with horses and stunt scenes. Comparing the two brothers, I personally find Kermit the more appealing as an action star, but fans at the time didn't agree, and he was eventually relegated to character roles in which he always turned in a fine job.

Johnny Mack Brown had started his screen career as a romantic leading man in big MGM silent productions, including *Our Dancing Daughters* and *Divine Woman* in 1928, but was discarded from the giant studio, rumor has it, when he began to pay too much attention to Marion Davies, who was then the exclusive property of William Randolph Hearst. Johnny found himself out in the cold and decided to become a Western actor, succeeding admirably in his ambition. He became a tremendous popular favorite at Universal, where he made both serials like *Wild West Days* and *Flaming Frontiers,* and numerous features both singly and on occasion paired with stars like Tex Ritter and Bob Baker. As a Western star he was one of the most convincing of the breed. When he threw a fake punch he gave it everything he had, convincing the audience that he was really connecting.

Warner Baxter, a really first-rate actor, brought two great Latin characters to the screen in the persons of the Cisco Kid and Joaquin Murrieta.

48

Given the professional polish expected from major studios, the Cisco Kid films from Twentieth Century-Fox and the Murrieta portrayal for MGM were tight little programmers that were a decided cut above the lesser B-Westerns, but which should be included in our survey just for the record.

Other stars who made final top-billed appearances or who were in series that would endure for only moderate runs included Wally Wales, who went on to continued success not as a leading man but as character actor Hal Taliaferro; Rex Lease, who performed similar duty and who can be found appearing in literally hundreds of roles in Westerns during the thirties and forties; Jack Perrin, who was to pop up in bit roles which were a far cry from his starring days; Bob Allen, who was a fine performer and gave many excellent performances, but who just didn't have enough magnetism to survive in the celluloid jungle; Reb Russell, whom I don't want to even think about because he was so awful; Jack Luden, who wasn't much better; Lane Chandler, whom I have always liked and who has lasted until today as an excellent character actor (remember him as one of the suspects for being the masked man in the serial *The Lone Ranger*?); Bill Cody, who, like Perrin, had star billing but not star quality; Yakima Canutt, who eschewed stardom in favor of becoming one of the greatest stuntmen the screen has ever known; and additional once-great favorites like Bob Custer, Guinn "Big

Boy" Williams, Buddy Roosevelt, Art Mix, Jack Hoxie, William Farnum, Jack Holt, Edmund Cobb and probably a dozen or more others that I am sure I have unintentionally overlooked. (Remember John Preston as Morton of the Mounted, folks?) There were even Westerns that featured a female lead, Dorothy Page, in titles like *Water Rustlers* and *The Singing Cowgirl*.

Additional Western favorites who started their illustrious saddle careers in the thirties, some as stars and others as supporting players, were Charles Starrett, who made a long string of successful outdoor films long before he became known only as the popular Durango Kid, wearing the black outfit and mask; Buster Crabbe, who played good guys, bad guys, Indians, and what-have-you; Dave O'Brien, who not only acted but did a good deal of stunt work; William Elliott, who started by playing fancy-dressed dudes and worked his way into becoming a popular favorite in Westerns and serials at Columbia; Donald Barry, who was doing minor roles in preparation for his forthcoming screen stardom; Allen Lane, whose screen career really went back to the beginning of the thirties; and Tim Holt, who started his Western career right at the close of this prolific decade. There were giant stars, minor greats, so-so players, and complete duds. Whatever your particular appetite demanded, this third decade of the B-Western had something or someone who was bound to satisfy you.

William Boyd finds a mortally wounded George Chesebro and is off on another Hopalong Cassidy adventure, this one called *Borderland* (Paramount 1937).

A scene from one of George O'Brien's excellent Fox films, *The Golden West* (Fox 1932). That's Stanley Blystone as a sullen army officer.

Tom London, *left*, and LeRoy Mason give George O'Brien a hard time in this scene from *The Border Patrolman* (Fox 1936).

Another picturesque scene, this time with George O'Brien and Cecilia Parker in *The Rainbow Trail* (Fox 1932).

A publicity shot of Tex Ritter, one of Gene Autry's main competitors in the saddle serenaders' derby in the late thirties.

Tex Ritter and Kenne Duncan in a scene from *Roll, Wagons, Roll* (Monogram 1939).

Dave O'Brien is about to give Jack Randall (Robert Livingston's brother in real life)
a bit of a headache in this scene from *Driftin' Westward* (Monogram 1939).

Veteran badman Harry Woods, *left*, seems impressed by Charles Starrett's fancy gunplay in *Gallant Defender* (Columbia 1935). This film is also noteworthy because a young member of the Sons of the Pioneers singing group, which appeared in the film, was the as yet undiscovered Roy Rogers.

Dick Foran, the Singing Cowboy, squares off against Harry Woods in this scene from *Land Beyond the Law* (Warner Bros 1937).

Dick Foran takes on Edmund Cobb in this wrestling match featured in *Cherokee Strip* (Warner Bros 1937).

Fred Scott was another very likable singing cowboy of the thirties.

Bob Baker, *left*, another thrush of the saddle, serenades his comical sidekick Fuzzy Knight in *Border Wolves* (Universal 1938).

Smith Ballew made a few features like *Roll Along, Cowboy* (Twentieth Century-Fox 1937) as another sagebrush troubadour, but was an unsuccessful competitor in the singing sweepstakes.

Kermit Maynard, Ken's younger brother and an excellent rider and stuntman, made a very entertaining string of adventure films in the mid-thirties. *His Fighting Blood* (Ambassador 1935) with Paul Fix, from which this scene is taken, was one of the better entries.

Ray Whitley, *center*, was the sidekick of a number of Western favorites like Tim Holt and Rod Cameron and also made a number of two-reel musical Westerns such as *Cupid Rides the Range* (RKO 1939) with Elvira Rios and Glenn Strange, from which this scene is taken.

Tom Keene (also known in films as George Duryea and Richard Powers at various times) in a striking scene from *Under Strange Flags* (Crescent 1938).

Tom Keene, *left*, does battle with veteran villain and
onetime star Monte Blue in *Desert Gold* (Paramount
1936), a film starring Buster Crabbe.

Rex Bell gives Bud Osborne a good going-over in
The Diamond Trail (Monogram 1933).

Johnny Mack Brown and Frances Robinson in *Desperate Trails* (Universal 1939).

Rex Bell, who eventually became Lieutenant Governor of Nevada and who was married to Clara Bow, here shown with Luana Walters in a scene from *Fighting Texans* (Monogram 1933).

Anthony Warde, *left*, in one of his few Western roles, seen with Johnny Mack Brown in *Oklahoma Frontier* (Universal 1939).

Warner Baxter, *center*, as the Cisco Kid, with Cesar Romero, *left*, who was himself later to play Cisco, and Chris Pin Martin as Pancho in *The Return of the Cisco Kid* (Twentieth Century-Fox 1939).

Bob Allen is in the fancy duds, and smiling at pal Hal Taliaferro in *Law of the Ranger* (Columbia 1937).

One of the real losers in the Western sweepstakes was Reb Russell, here with Mary Jane Carey in *Border Vengeance* (Willis Kent 1935).

While making *Robin Hood of El Dorado* (MGM 1936), Warner Baxter, playing the role of Joaquin Murrieta, had a visit from the prolific writer Peter B. Kyne, whose name probably appeared in more screenwriting credits than any other writer's during the period.

Rex Lease, *right*, makes a point with veteran cowboy star William Desmond in *Cyclone of the Saddle* (Superior 1935).

Wally Wales (later Hal Taliaferro) in a posed romantic interlude from *Breed of the West* (Big-4 1930).

How many people remember John Preston as Morton of the Mounted in *Timber Terrors* (Stage and Screen 1935)? That's Captain, King of Dogs, and Dynamite, the Wonder Horse, sharing this scene.

Robert Livingston brought his considerable talent to *The Bold Caballero* (Republic 1936), in which he played Zorro, the masked avenger. This film was Republic's first color film.

Dorothy Page, the Singing Cowgirl, gives Dave O'Brien some helpful hints in *Water Rustlers* (Grand National 1939).

Art Jarrett, Lee Powell (who was originally billed as Lee "Lone Ranger" Powell in the advertising, but was eventually forced by the copyright owners to cease and desist) and Al St. John in *Trigger Pals* (Grand National 1939).

Joan Barclay, Tex Fletcher (the Lonely Cowboy), and Ted Adams in *Six-Gun Rhythm* (Grand National 1939).

Roy Barcroft in one of my favorite portraits, from
King of the Texas Rangers (Republic 1941). Roy
had appeared in films made for many studios, but
was signed to an exclusive ten-year contract by
Republic in 1943.

5

THE DEVIL'S HENCHMEN

Although the audience's attention was primarily focused, quite naturally, on the incredible screen exploits of our favorite Western heroes, much of the success and popularity of those hour-long adventure films was directly attributable to the fine performances turned in by an excellent stock company of actors who played the heavies. One of the real pleasures most of us relished in those Saturday afternoon orgies was watching how increasingly despicable a Roy Barcroft, Kenne Duncan, Bud Geary, or Charles King could be from week to week. Space doesn't permit mention of the complete roster of this cinematic Legion of the Damned, but I would like to single out some particular favorites who brought considerable pleasure to Western movie-goers over the years.

Of all the black-hearted devils who specialized in outdoor mayhem, none looked more convincing on screen or handled his acting chores with more consummate skill than Roy Barcroft. Roy had broken into films in the early thirties doing bit parts and walk-ons (he was in Garbo's *Mata Hari*), but it wasn't until the late thirties that he began to come into his own. Harry Woods, one of the best of the badmen of the twenties and thirties, was the reigning lead heavy and Roy, who admired him greatly, frankly admitted modeling his screen characterizations after those of his idol. Alternating for several years among Columbia, Monogram, Universal, and other studios, Roy signed an exclusive ten-year contract with Republic in 1943

and became the new champion of villainy, reigning for over a decade. His versatility over the years found him doing Westerns, serials, dramas, comedies, musicals (remember him as the sheriff in *Oklahoma!*?). Then he transferred his skills to television, where he matured even further as a fine character actor. Off-screen, Roy was one of the nicest men one would ever want to meet, and I have never heard a single derogatory word ever uttered about him from the people he worked with (an extremely rare tribute, for there were plenty of bad things said about, oddly enough, the "heroes" in his films). Having a terrific sense of humor, Roy was a typical practical joker on the set, and on more than one occasion Don "Red" Barry, Bill Elliott or Allan Lane might have found their prized hair pieces (yes, they all wore frontal pieces to give them a more picturesque hair-line for the big screen) temporarily hidden by the playful bad guy. There was seldom any question in Roy's mind as to what type of role he was going to play when he received his latest script; it was very likely Sloan Nibley, a fine writer who turned out many screenplays for Republic and who is married to serial queen Linda Stirling, who originated the story of seeing Roy emerging from an office with a copy of his latest script and asking him, "Well, Roy, who is it this time? Ferguson or Slade?" to which Roy winked and replied, "Ferguson, of *course*." His mold was permanently cast.

Tom London's screen career began in the

days of *The Great Train Robbery* and continued without letup until the fifties. Another extremely versatile performer, he alternated between playing good and bad roles. Strictly cast as himself he made an excellent "brains" heavy, assigning other men to do his dirty work. With his hair whitened a little, he was the perfect heroine's father or ranch owner; his teeth out, he was a lovable old codger or happy sidekick. In superb physical shape (and quite a ladies' man off-screen even in his seventies), he was still able to ride, fight and jump around long after many of the heroes he had faced had passed from screen favor or died. Tom was another actor who was not limited strictly to the programmers; he could be found in big-budget productions as well (he played the man Katy Jurado sold her property to in the classic *High Noon*).

Trevor Bardette was quite similar to London in that he could play a wide range of roles. One of his favorite characterizations was that of the good bad man (originated in silent films by William S. Hart) who, after taking a small fling at chicanery, eventually redeems himself by sacrificing his life to save that of the hero. In *Marshal of Cripple Creek* he returned from spending time in prison to find his son following in his evil footsteps. After administering a fatherly beating, Bardette saved the boy from participating in a hold-up at the cost of his own life. When Bardette wanted to be really mean, however, he was cast in a role like that of the mysterious outlaw leader, Pegleg, in the serial *Overland with Kit Carson*.

Jack Ingram had hundreds of credits from the thirties and forties in which he was usually cast as one of the action heavies. Off-screen he was virtually a millionaire; he had parlayed his screen earnings through wise investments. Bud Geary could be seen in dozens of small roles in Twentieth Century-Fox films before he moved over to do duty mainly at Republic. An excellent stuntman, Geary handled much of his own fight work and riding. He was killed in an auto accident at the peak of his forties popularity.

Kenne Duncan, for a time, was getting more publicity than Roy Barcroft as the screen's greatest Western menace. Republic used him primarily as an action heavy, but when he moved to Columbia he got better and bigger roles in many of the Gene Autry features, and he made many television appearances. One of his highly publicized exploits was his trip to Japan, where he was

photographed riding Emperor Hirohito's famous white horse. Off-screen Kenne was one of Roy Barcroft's closest friends. Bob Kortman was another successful carry-over from the silent days who made hundreds of appearances as an exceptionally convincing badman. Not only could he portray the usual shifty-eyed gunslinger, but in the thirties he often played Indian roles in features as well as numerous serials. Richard Alexander was a heavy-set player who is now best remembered for playing Prince Barin in the first *Flash Gordon* serial, but his real forte was Western banditry, and though now well on in years he still makes an occasional screen appearance as an extra. Ed Cassidy and Jack Rockwell both had impressive careers as badmen but are even more identified with the other side of the law. Between the two of them they have probably played the sheriff role more than any ten other actors in B-Western history. George J. Lewis has had one of those odd movie careers that found him alternating between playing good guys and bad guys, with an occasional Indian role thrown in for good measure. He started out as a hero in silent films and early sound serials. By the time the forties came around, he was one of Republic's best action heavies, and he made numerous serials as a thoroughly blackhearted villain with few redeeming qualities. Right in the middle of this glorious period of skulduggery, they cast George as Linda Stirling's leading man in *Zorro's Black Whip*, and he was extremely effective in this to him welcome change of pace. Unfortunately, he was back to his standard roles all too soon, and remained playing basically evil men until he had matured into better character roles. For a while he was playing in the television Zorro series and an occasional feature film, but is now quite happily retired from the screen. William Haade was one of those strange character actors who could play the meanest villain in the world and still manage to make the character funny. In one Monte Hale film he went around making hilarious wisecracks as he calmly knifed to death numerous victims. At the same time he was able to also play extremely sympathetic roles, for example, the outlaw who robbed only because he needed money for his wife's operation.

Good "brains" heavies, those men who were out to win the West only for their own interests and sent out the likes of the aforementioned henchmen to do the dirty work, were well por-

70

Here's a fearsome foursome from *Daredevils of the West* (Republic 1943): William Haade, Robert Frazer, Ted Adams, and George J. Lewis.

trayed by men like Tristram Coffin, Robert Frazer, LeRoy Mason, Francis McDonald, Kenneth MacDonald, and others. Each of these actors had his own individual style while playing outlaw leaders, but each could readily find screen work on the opposite side of the law playing doctors, lawyers, ranchers, or what-have-you with equal skill.

And of course there were the stuntmen, that rugged group of daredevils who doubled both heroes and villains in the action sequences. Almost all of the best ones, Tom Steele, Dale Van Sickel, David Sharpe, Eddie Parker, Duke Green, Ken Terrell, and Fred Graham, played regular roles as henchmen. The most famous of all these men, of course, was Yakima Canutt, who played an endless variety of badmen in the thirties. Sometimes he would be the big boss out to thwart John Wayne or Bob Steele and their like, but most of the time he was just the lead gunslinger who spent six reels wiping out the good guys only to be bested before the final fade-out.

The list goes on and on: Ted Adams, Pierce Lyden, I. Stanford Jolley, Terry Frost, George Chesebro, Stanley Price, Hal Taliaferro, Mauritz Hugo, John Merton, Lane Bradford (Merton's real-life son), Morris Ankrum, Riley Hill, Marshall Reed, Forrest Taylor, Jack Kirk, Lane Chandler, Stanley Andrews, John Cason, Rex Lease, Robert Barron, Monte Blue, Carleton Young, Ray Teal, Robert Wilke, Glenn Strange (who made hundreds of Westerns but is better known for having played the Frankenstein Monster in several horror films), Edmund Cobb, and many more. I have tried throughout this book to include scenes which feature most of these men, but of necessity have had to omit some. But to all of them a vote of thanks for making our favorite Western heroes look so good on the screen.

Before ending this small chapter on villains, however, I must pay tribute to one special actor who was nearly everyone's choice as the favorite Western villain of all time, Charles King. It seemed that in almost every film you looked at in the thirties and early forties, there would be good old Charlie getting beaten up by Bob Steele or Hoot Gibson or Buck Jones or some other defender of justice. He'd be knocked over chairs, tables, bars, or stairs at the mere drop of an innuendo. As the years went on, King gained more weight, too much in fact, and eventually found himself playing the role of buffoon more than menace, to the chagrin of all of us. But Charles King had made his mark on screen history and in the memories of those of us who shared so many pleasant afternoons watching him die a hundred screen deaths he had so justly deserved.

Two grand old pros, Tom London, *left*, and Trevor Bardette in *Marshal of Cripple Creek* (Republic 1947).

George Chesebro and stuntman Eddie Parker in *Shadow Valley* (PRC 1947).

A trio of real menaces, Jack Ingram, Kenne Duncan, and Bud Geary, in *King of the Texas Rangers* (Republic 1941).

Edmund Cobb was a leading cowboy star in silent films and became a Western regular in films like *The Miracle Rider* (Mascot 1935).

Kenneth MacDonald was a favorite villain at Columbia, where he made films like *Valley of Vanishing Men* (Columbia 1942).

Jack Rockwell played sheriffs almost as often as
henchmen. This portrait is from *The Miracle Rider*
(Mascot 1935).

Jack Ingram played in hundreds of Westerns as an
action heavy. This pose is from *Zorro Rides Again*
(Republic 1937).

Another trio of bad hombres, Hal Taliaferro, Stanley
Price and, seated, Francis McDonald. Their plotting
in this scene from *Zorro's Black Whip* (Republic
1944) bodes evil to someone.

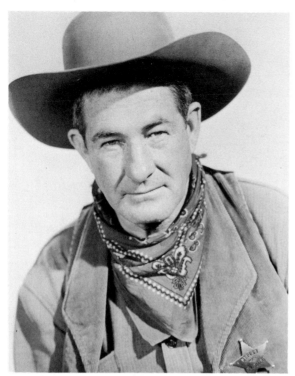

Fred Graham was a top stuntman, doubling frequently for John Wayne in big features, and played roles as a villain quite capably. This is a portrait from one of his late forties Republic features.

Edward Cassidy also specialized in playing sheriffs, but he was occasionally an outlaw. This portrait is from *Son of Zorro* (Republic 1947).

LeRoy Mason was a favorite "brains" heavy in films like *Vigilantes of Dodge City* (Republic 1944).

Roy Barcroft frequently had the assistance of top stuntman Tom Steele in films like *Ghost of Zorro* (Republic 1949).

Stuntman Dale Van Sickel, *left*, and Mauritz Hugo made a devilish twosome in *Man with the Steel Whip* (Republic 1954).

John Cason, *left*, and Lane Bradford (John Merton's real-life son), added to the villainy of many films like *Don Daredevil Rides Again* (Republic 1951).

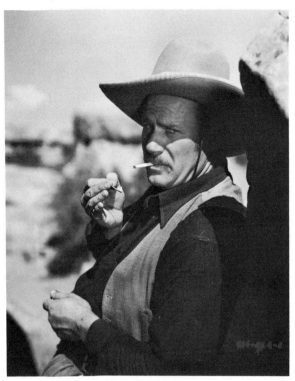

Dick Alexander was a favorite villain in the thirties and early forties. This is a portrait of him as the main action heavy in *Zorro Rides Again* (Republic 1937).

Harry Woods was a villain's villain, appearing in almost four decades of evil roles. Roy Barcroft admitted that he modeled his own screen image after that of Woods. This portrait is from one of Woods's later releases, *Short Grass* (Allied Artists 1950).

You couldn't get much meaner than the type of bad-man Bob Kortman usually was called upon to play. This scene is from *Zorro Rides Again* (Republic 1937).

Charles King played so many Western heavies that fans have long since lost count. Inasmuch as there are numerous pictures throughout the book with Charles as a bad guy, for a change of pace here is a scene of him in one of his zanier buffoon roles in *The Caravan Trail* (PRC 1946).

A publicity still for *The Lone Ranger* (Republic 1938). Any real Western fan worth his salt could spot, *left to right*, Lee Powell, George Letz (later Montgomery), Herman Brix (later Bruce Bennett), Lane Chandler, and Hal Taliaferro (formerly Wally Wales) behind those masks.

6

WINNING THE WEST
WEEK BY WEEK

The Western, more than any other subject matter, was ideally suited to the serial format. Here was an opportunity for the studios to showcase the talents of particular Western star favorites not only once every two or three months, but each and every week for twelve to fifteen consecutive Saturday afternoons. Producing serials also offered a great financial bonus to the studios, for they could take advantage of all the great natural perils Mother Nature had to offer without having to create elaborate studio cliffhangers. After all, building tall cliffs and waterfalls could be an expensive proposition (although Republic almost wound up doing just that near the end of their producing days, when it *was* cheaper to build inside than take loads of expensive equipment and large crews on actual location).

More than half of Mascot's serial output in the early thirties was devoted to Western adventures starring some of the biggest names of silent outdoor films. Some of them succeeded partially in being good action entertainment, but most of them missed the mark. All of them lacked real creativity, and rescreening of many of the better ones shows almost tedious repetition of long, seemingly endless chases with no musical backing to make them even tolerable. Tom Tyler starred in a lackluster effort called *Phantom of the West,* which was done in ten episodes. Supposedly a mystery, the real challenge to the audience was tolerating Tom's performance. It wasn't really his fault, how-

ever, for Tom was a talented performer who had done well in features. It was actually the fault of bad direction and poor scripting, as well as inferior supporting performances. Ken Maynard did a little better job in *Mystery Mountain,* supported by comic Syd Saylor. Another mystery, this film found the cowboy star battling a black-hooded and cloaked figure known as the Rattler. Tom Mix appeared in *The Miracle Rider,* his first serial and last film. Mix fans argue pro and con about this effort put forth by their hero. Many find him old, tired and completely uninspired in his performance. Others treat him in a more kindly light, but were disappointed that he didn't contribute more effort, as well as more footage, to the film. At best the whole thing could be described as mediocre. Harry Carey appeared in three serials for the studio: *The Vanishing Legion* (good), *The Last of the Mohicans* (bad) and *The Devil Horse* (indifferent). Carey was a fine actor, but he was simply too old for all the derring-do demanded by serial script requirements. Bob Custer and Johnny Mack Brown each appeared in a minor opus, but the one star who should have made a good Western serial, Bob Steele, found himself in an aviation adventure battling a mysterious enemy known as the Black Ace. The one really important Western serial to come from the studio was *The Phantom Empire.* Not only did the film serve to give Gene Autry his first leading role and push him on the road to eventual screen stardom, but it was a superior serial adventure to boot. Gene was a singing cowboy who found himself embroiled in intrigue which led him to a mysterious underground city called Murania. Besides the standard horse-opera heroics, audiences were now treated to science-fiction escapism almost a full year before Universal was to unreel *Flash Gordon.* It might be of interest to note here that two of Republic's best technicians were involved with this film, as well as other Mascot projects, even in those days. Howard Lydecker, who did not receive screen credit until the forties, was providing special effects for Mascot, and Bud Thackery, one of the best cameramen in the business, was doing glass shots (painting special effects on glass to be placed in front of the camera and photographed along with routine scenes to enhance a visual image), among other photographic work.

The most consistent fault found with Universal serials was the constant re-utilization of silent footage in virtually all of their talking productions. Time after time the same Indians were seen being shot from the same horses in the same attacks. Not only were similar scenes used in different serials, but often they were repeated in the same serial and occasionally even in the same chapter. Economy, of course, has its place, but there are limits, and taking old mismatched footage only antagonized audiences who were jarred when they saw the grainy, jerkily reproduced scenes pop up where their current heroes should have been in evidence. Almost one-third of Universal's total serial output was devoted to Western or pseudo-Western (Northwest Mounted Police, etc.) adventures. Buck Jones starred in *Gordon of Ghost City, The Red Rider, The Roaring West, The Phantom Rider* and *Riders of Death Valley* with varying degrees of success. The earlier ventures were slightly more interesting and contained better original footage, while an effort like *The Phantom Rider* turned into an almost complete bore. Ranking close to Buck in Universal serial popularity was Johnny Mack Brown, who starred in four episodic treats: *The Rustlers of Red Dog, Wild West Days, Flaming Frontiers,* and *The Oregon Trail.* The comments on Jones's films are likewise applicable to Brown's, with the distinction that Johnny, being considerably younger, was able to handle more of his own action chores. Dick Foran, who made an entertaining series of B-Westerns for Warner Bros and subsequently made many features at Universal, was

called upon for serial duty only twice. He was the star of the "Million Dollar Serial," *Riders of Death Valley*, which also featured Jones, Noah Beery, Jr., Leo Carrillo, Guinn "Big Boy" Williams, Charles Bickford, and Lon Chaney, Jr. (a routine effort except for the exceptional cast), and *Winners of the West*, an entertaining Western about railroad-building that had, as usual, those same Indians from the silents making their interjected guest appearances. Other routine efforts included Tim McCoy's *The Indians Are Coming* (the very first talking serial); Tom Tyler in *Battling with Buffalo Bill* and *Clancy of the Mounted* (as well as several non-Western serials); *Heroes of the West* with Noah Beery, Jr., and Onslow Stevens; Lon Chaney, Jr. in *Overland Mail* (which, oddly enough, was one of the studio's better Western serials); *Raiders of Ghost City* with Dennis Moore battling a frequently camera-mugging Lionel Atwill; Bill Kennedy in *The Royal Mounted Rides Again*; and Peter Cookson as the routine hero of *The Scarlet Horseman.* Universal was the first of the big three serial-producing companies to discontinue its chapter-play output, calling it quits in 1946 after turning out sixty-nine assorted adventures. Surely they could not claim that it was an economy move, since all of the films were filled with obvious cost-cutting short cuts. Therefore we must assume, as is frequently stated, that the studio simply wanted to divest itself of the B-film stamp in general and elevate its producing image to a more sophisticated level. To be quite honest, most people probably didn't miss them at all anyway.

The percentage of Western adventures turned out by Columbia serial makers was approximately the same as Universal's: almost thirty per cent. Columbia's were similarly filled with a considerable amount of stock footage, particularly as the product of the late forties and early fifties appeared. Unlike Universal, however, Columbia had few stars of any real magnitude. William Elliott was the most popular, appearing in *The Great Adventures of Wild Bill Hickock, Overland with Kit Carson,* and *The Valley of Vanishing Men.* Elliott was an exceptionally appealing performer, excelling both in dialogue delivery and action sequences, and he became one of Columbia's better all-around Western heroes. When he moved over to Republic, again to receive high popular acceptance, he made no serial appearances, and many of his fans felt shortchanged. The Columbia Elliott serials had a considerable amount of action, but it was generally misdirected. In *Overland with Kit Carson,* for example, every chapter contained an extended sequence in which the outlaws ambushed or otherwise confronted Elliott and fought a gun battle in which literally hundreds of shots were fired with hardly anyone ever being hit. Fortunately, the location photography was extremely picturesque and that was a redeeming quality the film really needed.

The remainder of the Columbia episodic oatburners varied according to the particular talents of the leading players. Don Douglas was an odd choice to play *Deadwood Dick,* but he had a good supporting cast including Roy Barcroft, Lorna Gray, and Lane Chandler, and a great many laughs were provided by inept lines of dialogue and bad staging. *White Eagle* had Buck Jones as its star, but was a very pedestrian effort. Buck had made an earlier feature for Columbia with the identical title, and stock from this was very much in evidence throughout the entire fifteen chapters. Ralph Byrd, taking time off from playing Dick Tracy, played the comic strip hero, *The Vigilante;* Robert Kellard, who had played the hero in Republic's popular *Drums of Fu Manchu,* performed a somewhat similar chore as Byrd had when he had the comic-strip lead in *Tex Granger* (earlier, using the name Robert Stevens, he had starred in *Perils of the Royal Mounted*); Jock Mahoney, who was a superb stuntman, did three later adventures that were built almost entirely around stock footage from earlier serials (*Cody of the Pony Express, Roar of the Iron Horse,* and *Gunfighters of the Northwest,* in which he did very little extraordinary original action work, to the dismay of all his loyal followers); Clayton Moore (who reaped a small fortune from playing the Lone Ranger on television and in two feature films made in color based on the character, and who continues to this very day making personal appearances as the masked man) was only so-so in *Son of Geronimo;* Marshall Reed, who once was considered to replace Bill Elliott in the Red Ryder series at Republic but lost out to Allan Lane, got a good chance to play a hero for a change in *Riding with Buffalo Bill,* but it advanced his career very little and Lee Roberts did extremely routine duty in Columbia's final Western serial adventure in 1956, *Blazing the Overland Trail.* Columbia serials were never intended to be examples of the studio's better product. They were made for

kids, and most of them contained the very same ingredients that went into the two-reel comedies that were being turned out at the same time. If any extraordinary elements of serial virtue emerged, it was usually quite by accident, or as the result of effort expended by an exceptional director like Spencer Gordon Bennet, who knew how to make serials that could please action fans.

Republic, as might be expected, turned out the very best action serials, and fully one-third of their entire output was devoted to outdoor adventures. Their most famous serial was *The Lone Ranger,* which came out in 1938. Extensive searching by numerous investigators have failed to turn up any sign of either this serial or its sequel, *The Lone Ranger Rides Again.* All records of the films have completely disappeared from Republic files; no negatives or prints have been located, and the new copyright owners can offer no information of any value concerning the properties. The mystery was even greater than the one audiences had to solve when they attempted to guess the real identity of the masked man from among five suspects when *The Lone Ranger* first appeared on Saturday matinee screens. A large budget was expended on bringing the famous radio show to the screen, and when Republic scriptwriters got hold of the property they rewrote it to conform to their own concepts rather than those of the radio scribes. What emerged was a slam-bang action serial that retained an element of mystery in determining who the real masked man was. The suspects were five men who all had moments of screen glory either before or after this film was released: George Letz later changed his name to George Montgomery and became a big star at Twentieth Century-Fox; Lane Chandler was a popular Western star and character actor, Hal Taliaferro had been a big cowboy draw as Wally Wales and now was a first-rate character actor; Herman Brix was one of the screen's Tarzans and gained later fame as a fine actor under his new name of Bruce Bennett; and Lee Powell, who had a fine career as a serial star and might have had an even greater one had he not died serving his country in World War II. The serial met with instant success and caused Republic to do a sequel the following year. *The Lone Ranger Rides Again,* dealing with the same hot property, should have been even better than the first, considering how much the quality of production had increased at Republic in a very short period of time—but it wasn't. A detailed study of the cutting continuity (a scene-for-scene breakdown of the entire film) shows it to be merely a routine Western adventure containing only the usual Republic chases, fights, etc. (Not that *that* was bad, by any means, but audiences expected much more considering the excellent quality of the first serial.) Robert Livingston played the masked rider of the plains and turned in his usual fine performance. Livingston, who had starred in *The Vigilantes Are Coming*, an earlier serial triumph from Republic, and the Three Mesquiteers series, was an extremely competent actor and a pleasure to watch on the screen. For numerous reasons he never attained the success or stardom in the forties which he deserved.

In addition to the two Lone Ranger serials, Republic turned out quite a number of immensely satisfying Western thrillers. There were several adventures based on the Zorro character: *Zorro Rides Again*, which had likable John Carroll singing and fighting his way against the villainy of Noah Beery and Dick Alexander; *Zorro's Fighting Legion*, with Reed Hadley turning in probably the best interpretation of the masked avenger as he battled the mysterious Don del Oro; *Zorro's Black Whip*, which made no mention of Zorro whatsoever in the entire serial but which did offer the considerable talents of Linda Stirling as the Whip and George J. Lewis (in a change of pace from his usual villainous roles) playing a very acceptable hero; *Son of Zorro*, in which George Turner and Peggy Stewart were out to trap a mysterious terrorist leader known only as the Boss; and *Ghost of Zorro*, with Clayton Moore (who al-

ternated between playing heroes and villains) playing the California protector in the last serial officially based on the character. Republic had long since mastered the Western format, and almost all of their serials contained more thrills in a single chapter than the features turned out by other studios offered in their entirety. *The Painted Stallion* had magnificent photography and an excellent Western cast headed by Ray "Crash" Corrigan, Hoot Gibson, Jack Perrin, and Hal Taliaferro; *Adventures of Red Ryder* introduced Don "Red" Barry to stardom and was chock-full of excellent footage contributed by David Sharpe, who doubled Barry in a great many of the action scenes; *King of the Texas Rangers* with "Slingin' Sammy" Baugh, the famous football star, turning in an extremely bad performance as an actor but a fine job as an action star; *King of the Royal Mounted, King of the Mounties,* and *Daredevils of the West* with Allan Lane slugging his way through chapter after chapter to contribute three great action classics to the Republic hall of action fame; *The Phantom Rider* with Robert Kent masquerading as an avenging Indian God; Clayton Moore glamorizing the famous outlaw in *Jesse James Rides Again* and *Adventures of Frank and Jesse James*; and an assortment of lesser vehicles turned out in the early fifties that utilized a great deal of excellent stock footage from earlier efforts.

It has been more than two decades since I made my last weekly journey to see my Western favorites serve up their own action-packed brand of justice, but the happy memories of those days can still be conjured up in my imagination whenever I choose to recall the thrill of it all!

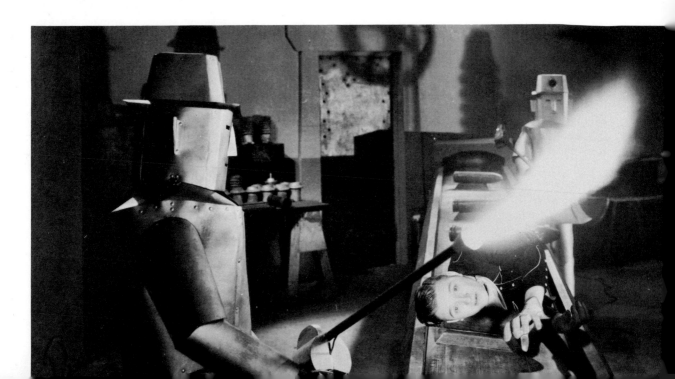

John Carroll played the dashing title character in *Zorro Rides Again* (Republic 1937).

This is one of the perils Gene Autry faced in *The Phantom Empire* (Mascot 1935).

The stars of *Heroes of the West* (Universal 1932) were Onslow Stevens, Martha Mattox, William Desmond, Diane Duval (who changed her name to Jacqueline Wells and then again to Julie Bishop) and Noah Beery, Jr.

Ken Maynard battles the mysterious Rattler in
Mystery Mountain (Mascot 1934).

George Brent and a descendant of Rin-Tin-Tin in
Lightning Warrior (Mascot 1931).

Popular favorite Harry Carey and young Frankie Darro in *The Devil Horse* (Mascot
1932).

Bob Custer takes care of Richard Alexander in
Law of the Wild (Mascot 1934).

"Slingin' Sammy" Baugh, the great football star, and Duncan Renaldo, *right*, in
King of the Texas Rangers (Republic 1941).

Buck Jones in a portrait from *White Eagle* (Columbia 1941).

Trevor Bardette was the grotesque villain in *Overland with Kit Carson* (Columbia 1939).

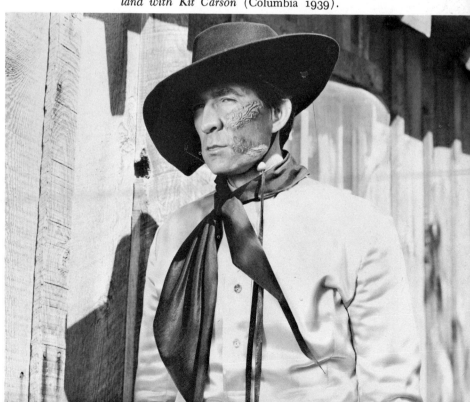

Lane Chandler, *center*, was the third to die of the five suspects for being the masked hero. Herman Brix, *left*, and Lee Powell remained as the closing chapters of *The Lone Ranger* (Republic 1938) approached.

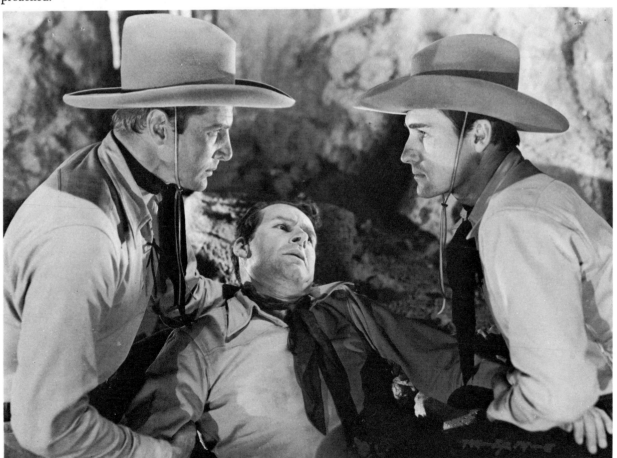

Lee Powell and Chief Thunder-cloud as the Lone Ranger and Tonto in the first serial
version featuring the famous characters, *The Lone Ranger* (Republic 1938).

William Elliott, seen here with Iron Eyes Cody, was the star of *Overland with Kit Carson* (Columbia 1939).

Don Douglas was the masked hero of *Deadwood Dick* (Columbia 1940). Edmund Cobb is giving him a little help here.

Chief Thunder-cloud and Robert Livingston face
a chapter-ending peril in *The Lone Ranger Rides
Again* (Republic 1939), the second, and final, serial
based on the famous radio character.

Robert Livingston unmasked in *The Lone Ranger
Rides Again* (Republic 1939).

Robert Livingston masked in *The Lone Ranger
Rides Again* (Republic 1939).

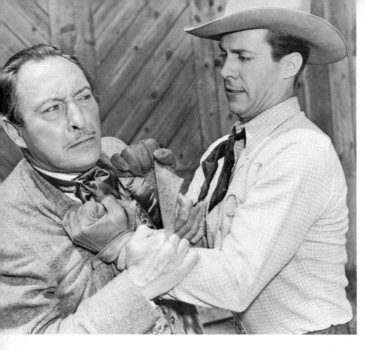

Dennis Moore gives a justly deserved beating to Lionel Atwill, *left*, in *Raiders of Ghost City* (Universal 1944).

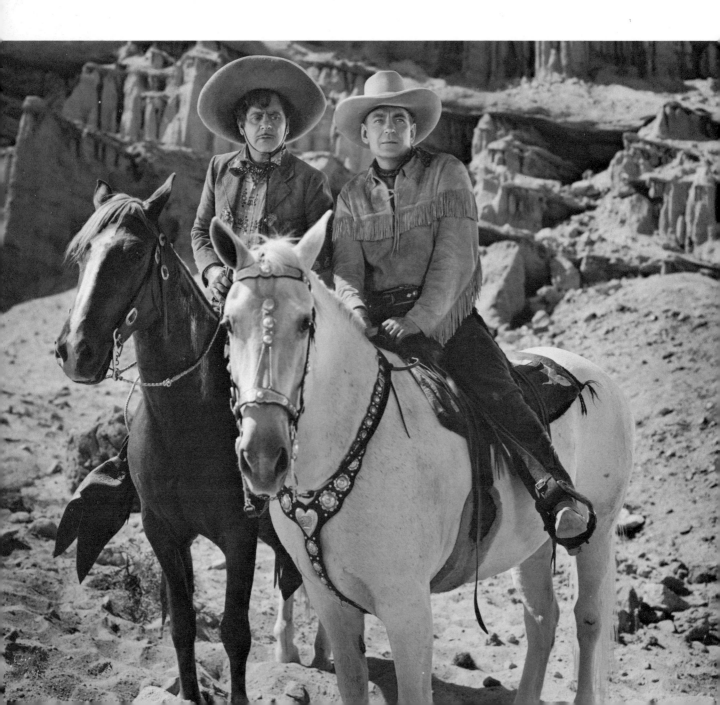

Don Terry, Lon Chaney, Jr., and Noah Beery, Jr., were the stars of *Overland Mail*. (Universal 1942).

Leo Carrillo and Buck Jones in the "Million Dollar Serial" *Riders of Death Valley* (Universal 1941), a grossly over-rated and over-publicized serial whose only real merit was the large star-laden cast.

Johnny Mack Brown in *Rustlers of Red Dog* (Universal 1935).

Don "Red" Barry, *right*, as Red Ryder delivers one to the chin of Bud Geary in *Adventures of Red Ryder* (Republic 1940).

James Pierce, *center*, and Charles King force the masked Reed Hadley into a deadly trap in *Zorro's Fighting Legion* (Republic 1939).

Tom Mix's final film was the serial *The Miracle Rider* (Mascot 1935). Here he appears with Edward Hearn in a scene from the film.

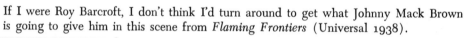

If I were Roy Barcroft, I don't think I'd turn around to get what Johnny Mack Brown is going to give him in this scene from *Flaming Frontiers* (Universal 1938).

A romantic scene you can bet serial fans would never see on the screen, a publicity shot for *Zorro's Black Whip* (Republic 1944) with Linda Stirling and George J. Lewis.

Maston Williams appears to have star Ray Corrigan at a decided disadvantage in this picturesque scene from *The Painted Stallion* (Republic 1937).

Other Western favorites who appeared in *The Painted Stallion* (Republic 1937) were Hal Taliaferro (formerly Wally Wales), Hoot Gibson, and Jack Perrin.

Tom London wants to make sure that Allan Lane is well done in the action-packed *Daredevils of the West* (Republic 1943).

Robert Kent, *right*, masked as *The Phantom Rider* (Republic 1946), rescues Peggy Stewart from villain-stuntman Dale Van Sickel.

Extraordinary stuntman-actor Jock Mahoney, *left*, was the star of *Cody of the Pony Express* (Columbia 1950). That's veteran character actor Tom London, *left*, and Dickie Moore showing Jock an important clue.

7

TRIGGER TRIOS

Prior to the middle thirties, audience attention at Saturday matinees was focused primarily on the exploits of a single Western hero, with the occasional assistance of a comical sidekick. Popular Western author William Colt MacDonald changed all that in 1935 when he wrote a story called *Law of the 45's*. This story was the written introduction of Tucson Smith, Stoney Brooke, and Lullaby Joslin, who called themselves the Three Mesquiteers, a Western version of the famous Three Musketeers. That same year the story was brought to the screen by Normandy Films with Guinn "Big Boy" Williams playing Tucson Smith and silent screen comedian Al St. John playing Stoney Brooke. Lullaby, for some reason, was eliminated from the screenplay. The film had some action, but is really only remembered because it was the first to introduce the now-famous characters.

That same year the real granddaddy of all the Three Mesquiteer films was made over at RKO. *Powdersmoke Range* was billed as "The Barnum and Bailey of Westerns" and featured, in addition to top-billed Harry Carey and Hoot Gibson, the greatest cast of Western "greats" ever brought together for a single film: Bob Steele, Tom Tyler, Guinn Williams, William Farnum, William Desmond, Buzz Barton, Wally Wales, Art Mix, Buffalo Bill, Jr., Buddy Roosevelt, and Franklyn Farnum. Williams played Lullaby Joslin with Carey as Tucson Smith and Gibson as Stoney Brooke. Tom Tyler, usually cast as a true-blue hero, played a sympathetic

villain who wound up getting killed in a moving screen sequence.

A year later Republic became interested in the characters and bought the rights. With Robert Livingston as Stoney, Ray Corrigan as Tucson, and Max Terhune as Lullaby, the studio turned out sixteen films in a two-year period. In the first film of the series, *The Three Mesquiteers*, comic Syd Saylor played Lullaby, and in the tenth, *Trigger Trio*, Ralph Byrd replaced a temporarily ailing Livingston. Aside from those two minor switches the cast remained intact, and the series became a big money-maker for the growing Republic organization. The chemistry among the players was ideal. Livingston was perfect as the fun-loving, wisecracking, devil-may-care saddle ace who was always getting into trouble. Corrigan was similarly effective as the rugged individualist who was always getting his partner out of jams, and the comedy of Max Terhune with his dummy, Elmer, was always easy to take compared with the silliness of some screen sidekicks. The films varied considerably in quality and interest. *The Riders of the Whistling Skull* was a most unusual Western which found the Mesquiteers joining an expedition that was searching for a lost tribe and was being decimated by a mysterious killer. *Hit the Saddle* was unusual in that the young lady Livingston lost his heart to, and hoped to marry until Corrigan broke them up, was young Rita Cansino, who later changed her name to Hayworth and danced her way to screen immortality. My favorite film in the series was *Heart of the Rockies,* in which the three heroes were out to trap a bunch of animal poachers who were killing creatures on an off-limits preserve. Location photography was topnotch, and there was an excellent chase as well as an exciting fight between Livingston and Yakima Canutt.

After the sixteenth film the studio decided to move Livingston to better quality features and brought John Wayne, who had worked for the studio earlier, back to do a series of eight Mesquiteer films with Corrigan and Terhune. All eight of these films had a slickness and quality that made them rank among the very best films turned out by the studio. Almost all of them had excellent background scores with music composed especially for serials and features by, among others, William Lava.

When Wayne departed after his success in *Stagecoach,* which he made during the same period as the Mesquiteer films, Republic brought Livingston back and paired him up with Duncan Renaldo and Raymond Hatton in another series of seven titles. During 1939 Livingston had appeared in the serial *The Lone Ranger Rides Again,* a popular though uninspired sequel to the hit serial *The Lone Ranger* made a year previous. As though to use the Lone Ranger image without actually using the name, Republic had Livingston don a somewhat similar mask and ride the same kind of white horse throughout the seven films. The gimmick was a good one, and the films are immensely satisfying. Another seven-title series followed with Bob Steele replacing Duncan Renaldo and Rufe Davis subbing for Raymond Hatton; this was a little less satisfying, though still quite enjoyable. Another year passed and Republic then brought Tom Tyler in to replace Livingston for another seven films, and then, finally, the series completely ended with a final six films in which Jimmy Dodd replaced Davis and joined Tyler and Steele in some completely lackluster programmers. In all the studio had produced a total of fifty-one films in the popular series that finally ended in May of 1943.

Over at Monogram in the forties there were three very popular series which featured fighting trios. The most popular of these was, of course, the Rough Riders series, composed of eight films made in the 1941–1942 season, *Arizona Bound, Gunman from Bodie, Forbidden Trails, Below the Border, Ghost Town Law, Down Texas Way, Riders of the West,* and

West of the Law. Starring Buck Jones, Tim McCoy, and Raymond Hatton, all eight films were real audience pleasers. Frequently the plots would tend to be somewhat similar, with Buck usually masquerading as a bandit or some other kind of social outcast in order to work his way into the good graces of whatever gang they were currently trying to bust up. Hatton played Sandy Hopkins, a character he carried over into his features with Johnny Mack Brown made at the same studio following this series. He usually sauntered into town as some kind of drifter looking for work, and Tim usually made his appearance dressed to the nines as a preacher, gambler, or other well-to-do gentleman. Eventually they all got together near the film's end and, after making up their plan of battle, shouted "Let's go, Rough Riders!" and rode off at a spirited pace to do battle with the likes of Charlie King or Roy Barcroft. Remember Buck's favorite gimmick in the series? Whenever he was getting annoyed he would pop a piece of chewing gum into his mouth. I remember how, as children, we used to jump up and down in our seats and start screaming our approval the minute we saw him go for that shirt pocket where we knew he kept that gum. Although Monogram musical scores were of a far lower caliber than Republic's, the background tracks for the Rough Riders films were a cut above the norm and were generally pleasing. All the films opened with a spirited "Rough Riders Song" sung over the main titles, and the finale of each found Buck, Tim, and Ray calling out "So long, Rough Riders" as they rode down a trail and then branched off into separate directions, again with the vocal theme in the background.

At the end of the series McCoy went into the armed forces to do World War II duty in a special capacity and the studio brought in Rex Bell to join Buck and Ray in a new string of features beginning with *Dawn on the Great Divide.* Buck wore a completely new outfit, composed of more buckskin and less denim, and looked exceptionally good, but the series died a premature death when Jones was killed in the tragic Coconut Grove fire while in the midst of a U.S. War Bond selling tour. I remember Roy Barcroft, who was one of the featured heavies in *Dawn,* telling me that when the cast went in to see the final rough cut of the film that "there wasn't a dry eye in the place and especially mine." Monogram brought Johnny

Buck Jones, Raymond Hatton, and Tim McCoy were the stars of the popular Monogram series in which they called themselves the Rough Riders.

Mack Brown over from Universal to fill the void with his almost decade-long series of actioners.

When Ray Corrigan left the Three Mesquiteers series at Republic it was with the intention of producing his own independent productions. He brought Max Terhune along with him and added John King, thus forming his own new trio, which he called the Range Busters. Distributed by Monogram, the Range Busters Westerns, though decidedly not of the superior quality of the Republic films, were entertaining and found popular acceptance. In all there were twenty-four films made in the series, which appeared on screen between 1940 and 1942. Terhune, who was called "Alibi" as opposed to his previous "Lullaby" as a Mesquiteer, was in all of the films, while Corrigan, nicknamed "Crash," and King, nicknamed "Dusty," survived until the final few films when Dennis Moore and ace stuntman David Sharpe were called in to assist in the last four titles. In *Haunted Ranch* Sharpe disappeared right in the middle of the film because he had to go into the armed forces before shooting could be completed. It was explained in the film that he had left "to join Teddy Roosevelt's Rough Riders." Veteran Rex Lease was brought in to finish the film. My favorite films in the series were *The Trail of the Silver Spur*, in which I. Stanford Jolley gave an excellent performance as the man who wore those titled spurs, and *Saddle Mountain Round-up*, which was an exciting murder mystery yarn with veteran Jack Mulhall giving an interesting portrayal.

The third series turned out by Monogram was the Trail Blazers films, which featured a notable group of performers appearing in various combinations. Ken Maynard, Hoot Gibson, and Bob Steele appeared in *Death Valley Rangers, Westward Bound,* and *Arizona Whirlwind* with so-so results. The films had a considerable amount of action, especially in the finales, which seemed to have an almost endless barrage of shots being fired. Steele, still in excellent shape, gave the best performances, while Hoot and Ken, fat and well past his prime, offered more nostalgia than anything else. Prior to these three films Ken and Hoot had teamed up to do *Wild Horse Stampede, The Law Rides Again* and *Blazing Guns,* and after the trio efforts Maynard dropped out and Hoot and Bob had Chief Thundercloud, who as Chief Thunder-cloud had played Tonto in the two Lone Ranger serials, join them for *Outlaw Trail* and *Sonora Stagecoach.* After that the Trail Blazers tag was dropped from the billing and Bob and Hoot finished their Monogram work with *Utah Kid, Marked Trails* and *Trigger Law.*

There were, of course, other groups; Dave O'Brien, James Newill, and Guy Wilkerson had called themselves the Texas Rangers, and often two stars, like Johnny Mack Brown and Bob Baker, or William Elliott and Tex Ritter, would be joined by a sidekick like Fuzzy Knight or Dub "Cannonball" Taylor, but generally when the true B-Western fan thinks of trigger trios it is the Three Mesquiteers, The Rough Riders, the Range Busters, or the Trail Blazers that come most readily to mind.

Bob Steele, Guinn "Big Boy" Williams, Hoot Gibson, Harry Carey, and Tom Tyler in the star-loaded Three Mesquiteer adventure, *Powdersmoke Range* (RKO 1935).

Harry Carey and Bob Steele in another scene from the granddaddy of all the Three Mesquiteer films, *Powdersmoke Range* (RKO 1935). Before all the experts rise up in alarm, however, I must add that *Law of the 45's* (Normandy 1935), based on William Colt MacDonald's original story, was actually the first real Mesquiteer opus; but the film version contained only *two* Mesquiteers, played by Guinn "Big Boy" Williams and Al St. John. So much for the purists.

Tom Tyler was on the wrong side in *Powdersmoke Range* (RKO 1935).

One last rare scene from *Powdersmoke Range* (RKO 1935) showing Guinn "Big Boy" Williams, veteran badman Ethan Laidlaw, Harry Carey, and Hoot Gibson. What a cast!

Max Terhune, *left*, and Ray Corrigan, *right*, successfully broke up Robert Livingston's engagement to lovely Rita Cansino (later, of course, Rita Hayworth) in the Three Mesquiteer adventure *Hit the Saddle* (Republic 1937).

Roy Barcroft, Ray Corrigan, LeRoy Mason, Max Terhune, and Bob Livingston in the Three Mesquiteer thriller, *Heroes of the Hills* (Republic 1938).

John Wayne, William Farnum, Ray Corrigan, and Max Terhune in *Santa Fe Stampede* (Republic 1938), another Three Mesquiteer adventure.

John Wayne and Raymond Hatton in *New Frontier* (Republic 1939), one more in the continuing Three Mesquiteer series.

Raymond Hatton, Duncan Renaldo, and Bob Livingston as another set of The Three Mesquiteers in *Pioneers of the West* (Republic 1940).

Bob Steele and Hoot Gibson in *Trigger Law* (Monogram 1944).

Bob Livingston is behind that mask in *Covered Wagon Days* (Republic 1940). His Three Mesquiteer pals, Raymond Hatton and Duncan Renaldo, are also covered by gang leader George Douglas in the fancy duds.

Hoot Gibson, *left*, looks like he is about to make one of his wisecracks to Ian Keith while Ken Maynard keeps working on that safe in *Arizona Whirlwind* (Monogram 1944), one of the Trail Blazers adventures.

Bob Steele does a little clowning with the ever popular Veda Ann Borg in *Marked Trails* (Monogram 1944).

Young Don Stewart, Hoot Gibson, and Ken Maynard look approvingly at the fine work Bob Steele has done by besting George Chesebro in the Trail Blazers film *Arizona Whirlwind* (Monogram 1944).

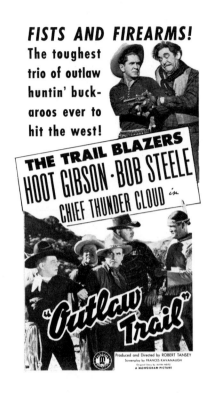

Bob Steele, Hoot Gibson, Chief Thundercloud, and Rocky Cameron in the Trail Blazers production *Outlaw Trail* (Monogram 1944).

Glenn Strange, *left*, and Tim McCoy enjoy Buck Jones's horseplay with pal Raymond
Hatton in *Down Texas Way* (Monogram 1942), a Rough Riders feature.

In the Rough Riders films Buck Jones, *right*, usually worked his way into the outlaw gangs he was trying to break up. In this scene from *West of the Law* (Monogram 1942) Buck pretty well has Roy Barcroft and Harry Woods, both standing, convinced that Tim McCoy is going to be taken care of in short order.

Buck Jones, Mona Barrie, and Roy Barcroft in Buck's last film before his untimely death, *Dawn on the Great Divide* (Monogram 1942).

Roy Barcroft loses out again to Buck Jones, this time in *Below the Border* (Monogram 1942), another Rough Riders film.

Buck Jones and Raymond Hatton in another scene from *Dawn on the Great Divide* (Monogram 1942).

Bob Steele riding hard and fast in one of his forties Three Mesquiteer adventures.

John "Dusty" King, Jack Mulhall, and Ray "Crash" Corrigan tried to solve a murder mystery in *Saddle Mountain Round-Up* (Monogram 1941), a Range Busters picture.

Guy Wilkerson, Dave O'Brien and James Newill called themselves the Texas Rangers in *Thundergap Outlaws* (PRC 1947), one in a series featuring the trio.

One of the last Range Busters films was *Two Fisted Justice* (Monogram 1943), with Max "Alibi" Terhune, David Sharpe, and John King playing the outlaw-busting trio.

The King of the Cowboys, Roy Rogers, and his queen, Dale Evans.

8

GUNS
AND GUITARS

It seems a bit incongruous that in a genre that depended primarily upon real he-man action and thrills from its stars two guitar-strumming, warbling saddle serenaders should become the reigning kings of the Western film empire in the late thirties and forties—but that is exactly what happened. Gene Autry and Roy Rogers both parlayed pleasant singing voices and winning personalities into public popularity unmatched since the early days of Tom Mix's phenomenal mass appeal.

Autry and Rogers both came up the hard way, earning their chance at screen stardom by serving singing apprenticeships for several years before getting their first movie breaks. Autry began his singing career at an early age in Tioga, Texas, where, as the grandson of a Baptist minister, he performed frequent choir service. As he matured he used his singing capabilities in a variety of ways, from singing on Saturday nights at a local restaurant to appearing in carney shows, where those famous patent medicines we saw in so many B-Western plots were actually hucstered. Eventually he wound up on a local radio station and was soon discovered by a Columbia Records scout and signed to a contract. He had an appealing voice and his recordings sold well. Along with Jimmy Long he wrote "That Silver-Haired Daddy of Mine" and his recording of that song made him famous. He became a regular feature of the National Barn Dance radio program, and film producer Nat Levine offered him a role as a singing cowboy in his Ken Maynard film *In Old Santa Fe*, made in 1934. In that film Gene sang only a few brief numbers, but it was enough to encourage the studio, Mascot Pictures, to feature him as the star of a way-out serial, *The Phantom Empire*, in which Gene played a singing cowboy who discovered a mysterious underground city called Murania and had numerous adventurous escapades. He also had a chance to sing "That Silver-Haired Daddy of Mine" every other chapter or so. The die was now cast. He was put into his own series of starring vehicles released by Republic Pictures, which was a new studio formed by an amalgamation of Mascot, Monogram, and Consolidated, and became a smash hit with his very first film, *Tumbling Tumbleweeds*, released in 1935. Between 1935 and 1947 he made a total of fifty-six features for Republic, each of which made a bundle of money for the studio's coffers. I have seen all of the films either in theaters or on television, and it is amazing to notice how vastly they varied in quality and entertainment value. The studio had a habit each year of turning out set series for each star, and in the case of Autry, and later Rogers, they would produce from four to six routine efforts and then spend considerable time and expense to do a few really big shows with glossier production numbers, more exotic locations, and more involved finales. No matter, though, for all the films seemed to be met with equal enthusiasm from fans both young and old.

Although many people prefer the earlier films, I frankly find that they do not quite hold up to the excitement generated in the later more polished efforts. True, there was more location work, but Gene was still awkward before the camera, and even in his best films from the period, like *Red River Valley* and *Yodelin' Kid from Pine Ridge,* he wasn't used to best advantage. I believe Autry's best years were 1939 to 1942, when he looked, acted, and sang his very best in *Mexicali Rose, Blue Montana Skies, South of the Border, Down Mexico Way,* and others. My favorite of all the Autry films is *Mexicali Rose.* It is not, by any means, one of his most action-packed films, but it is certainly one of his most pleasant. In addition to a fine, though slightly overdone, performance by Noah Beery as a Mexican bandit who loved Autry's singing, Gene sang two of his very best songs, the title number (one of his biggest record sellers ever) and "You're the Only Star in My Blue Heaven." Another personal favorite was his 1942 film *Home in Wyomin'* which was an exciting mystery-Western that kept you guessing until the final showdown in the famous Republic "cave" sets. Other popular Autry features at the studio included *Goldmine in the Sky,* the title of another one of his smash record hits, *Melody Ranch,* in which he shared the spotlight with Jimmy Durante and Ann Miller, *Springtime in the Rockies,* and *Man From Music Mountain.*

Right at the peak of his popularity in 1942 Gene enlisted in the Air Force to fight in World War II, and when he returned four years later he found that the studio had built Roy Rogers into its new king of the cowboys. Gene made one short series for Republic in 1946 and 1947 and then left the studio he had helped in no small measure to build and went into independent production where he turned out numerous films released by Columbia Pictures. In addition, he had a popular radio show sponsored by Wrigley's gum which ran for years, and when television came into its own he produced series which not only featured himself but Jock Mahoney (the Range Rider), Dick Jones (Buffalo Bill, Jr.), Gail Davis (Anne Oakley), and even his horse (Champion). For all his shortcomings, and he frankly admits many, such as the fact that he was not a good horseman and frequently found himself falling out of the saddle in his early days (in fact, one of the most embarrassing incidents in his life occurred during one of his famous Madison Square Garden rodeo appearances right after his return from war duty when, in front of a packed house, he slipped off Champion and fell right on his rear end), and the fact that it took him years to learn how to throw an effective screen punch so that his fight scenes wouldn't have to be done in long shots with an obvious double, he was still one of the most pleasing and successful Western stars in screen history.

Roy Rogers, who's real name was Leonard Slye, decided on a show business career early in life just as Autry had, and he headed out to California from his home in Ohio to try his luck. After much the same type of exposure as Autry had experienced—singing with groups and solo, and radio appearances on the Hollywood Barn Dance show—Roy made his entrance into films as a member of the Sons of the Pioneers singing group in an appearance in *The Old Homestead,* a 1935 film featuring Mary Carlisle. After that the group appeared in *Tumbling Tumbleweeds,* Autry's first starring feature, *Gallant Defender* and *The Mysterious Avenger,* two early Charles Starrett adventures at Columbia, and several other assorted titles. In Autry's 1938 film, *The Old Barn Dance,* he received billing as Dick Weston and had a featured, though small, part. Republic was impressed with the young man and decided to build him into a new series star, introducing him to movie audiences in *Under Western Stars.* The rest is history. From 1938 to 1942 the studio featured him in a continuing string of pleasant, but generally uninspired, period films set in the old West. It wasn't until Autry left the home studio range for the Air Force that Roy was put into elaborately-mounted vehicles that would catapult him into the number-one Western star spot, from which he was never to decline. Even today, twenty years after his last starring series film made for Republic Pictures, *Pals of the Golden West* in 1951, he still holds the title of King of the Cowboys and continues to make frequent appearances on television with his wife and frequent film co-star, Dale Evans.

The early Rogers films, unlike Autry's, did not utilize his vocal talents as much as his action capabilities. In fact, in some films he only sang one or two songs, whereas in some of Autry's there would be as many as eight. The young man looked good in the saddle, and many of the production people at the studio rated him in later years right alongside William Elliott and Don "Red" Barry as a topnotch horseman. He

126

Roy in his first starring feature, *Under Western Stars* (Republic 1938).

could also handle dialogue well, and, particularly in the late forties, he was able to manage much of his action work with a high degree of skill. Prior to *Heart of the Golden West,* which was his first big production film and which, incidentally, featured both Smiley Burnette and George "Gabby" Hayes in a rare joint appearance, Roy had made thirty-one starring feature Westerns, as well as appearing in isolated features like *Dark Command* and *Jeepers Creepers,* in a period of only a little over four years. The films had titles like *In Old Caliente, Saga of Death Valley, Colorado, The Arizona Kid,* and one was hard to distinguish from another. But now the studio really duded him up in fancy dress shirts, gave him elaborate production-number backing, photographed him in picturesque locations, and stretched the running times of his features from an average of slightly less than sixty minutes to over seventy, and on an extremely rare occasion like *Bells of San Angelo* over eighty minutes. For many years during this period the Rogers films were set in modern locales in the current West. (Autry's films had similarly bounced around between period Westerns and modern-day adventures.) My favorite Rogers film in that middle forties period was *Silver Spurs,* which featured John Carradine as the main villain and which was filmed in beautiful Sierra Nevada Mountain country. In addition to several pleasant songs, there were numerous action sequences, including a spectacular wagon chase which found stuntmen leaping from a wagon in midair as it plunged over a cliff into a lake far below.

It was in 1944's *The Cowboy and the Senorita* (Herbert Yates, for some silly reason, loved to use titles like The ——— and the ———; he once wanted to call his award winning *The Quiet Man* "The Prizefighter and the Colleen") that Dale Evans made her first important entrance in a Rogers picture, and she was thereafter to appear in more than twenty-five of Roy's later films.

After several years of these elaborate musical-Westerns, the studio began to bring in a new crop of writers who started to eliminate the musical nonsense and give Roy some strictly rugged action work to do. In *Bells of San Angelo,* writer Sloan Nibley had Roy beaten nearly to death on-screen by David Sharpe and Dale Van Sickel. Filmed at a picturesque mining site high in the mountains, *Bells* was full of red-blooded action of the kind we had not seen in Roy's earlier films. Although there were of necessity a few songs in each new title, they were kept to a minimum and Roy finished his feature film duty more as an action ace than a singing cowboy.

Again, like Autry, Roy wound up doing a very popular radio show and moving into television, where he made his own starring series of half-hour shows featuring Dale Evans and comic sidekick Pat Brady. Now he rests on his laurels and spends a great deal of time at his movie museum in Apple Valley, California, where, among such items as the original truck he first came to California in, you can find the stuffed form of his famous horse Trigger, which, although it may seen slightly grotesque, was done simply because Roy felt his fans loved Trigger so much that they would not wish to simply have him buried. Both he and Dale appear at fairs and on television whenever they feel inclined to do so, and the two extremely friendly stars are always more than pleased to talk to their many fans who visit the museum.

Between the two, Rogers and Autry made appearances in almost two hundred motion pictures—not bad at all for a couple of country boys who parlayed their voices and guitar-strumming into a movie goldmine.

Gene Autry is singing the title song in this scene from *Gold Mine in the Sky* (Republic 1938), one of his best films and most popular songs.

Roy gives Harry Woods a little aggravation in *The Ranger and the Lady* (Republic 1940) while George "Gabby" Hayes, Jacqueline Wells (later Julie Bishop), Ted Mapes, and Yakima Canutt look on.

130

Gerald Mohr, *center*, and James Bush catch Roy doing some snooping in *King of the Cowboys* (Republic 1943).

Gene exhibits a little riding skill in *Blue Montana Skies* (Republic 1939).

Roy and Dale Evans show Paul Harvey some important evidence in *Heldorado* (Republic 1946).

A nice portrait of Gene from his only non-Republic film between 1935 and 1947, *Shooting High* (Twentieth Century-Fox 1940).

Gene poses with Rudy Vallee at one of countless benefits stars of his caliber were required to attend. This one took place in 1939.

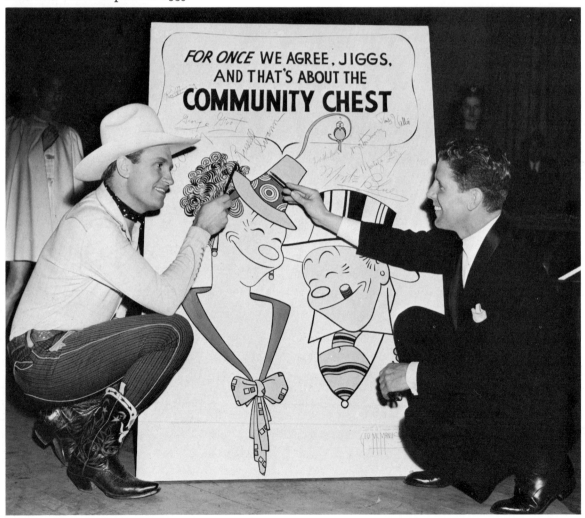

A portrait of Roy with his producer, Edward J. White, and director, William Witney, taken at a party given for Roy on his ninth anniversary as a Republic star.

Another scene at the same party shows Roy with William Elliott, studio head Herbert J. Yates, and Pat Buttram, who had made appearances on Roy's popular radio show.

Gene with Hamilton MacFadden and Kay Aldridge in *Shooting High* (Twentieth Century-Fox 1940).

Young Michael Chapin expressed in this picture what millions of fans probably had done in real life: admiration for Roy Rogers, the King of the Cowboys. This scene is from *Under California Stars* (Republic 1948).

Gene and Jimmy Durante in *Melody Ranch* (Republic 1940), another of Gene's very popular films.

Gene delivers one to the chin of Joe Sawyer in *Down Mexico Way* (Republic 1941).

Gene and wife Ina dress for another benefit. The Autrys are one of Hollywood's happiest and longest-married couples.

In a publicity shot, Gene visits briefly with former cowboy great Tom Tyler, who was in costume for his starring role in the serial *Adventures of Captain Marvel* (Republic 1941).

Roy and Dale look at the NBC listings showing the time of their popular radio program.
Serial fans, that name at the bottom, Knox Manning, belonged to the man who spoke
all those forewords to Columbia serials in the forties.

Gene and leading lady Peggy Stewart in *Trail to San Antone* (Republic 1947).

Gene with Jay Silverheels, who played Tonto to Clayton Moore's Lone Ranger, in one of his late forties releases, *The Cowboy and the Indians* (Columbia 1949).

Dale Van Sickel grabs Roy to begin a brutal fight sequence in *Bells of San Angelo* (Republic 1947), while Andy Devine, *left*, and David Sharpe, holding Roy's guns, look on.

Roy's personal favorite of all the films he made was *My Pal Trigger* (Republic 1946). In this scene he is surrounded by Bob Nolan, Karl Farr, Shug Fisher, Jack Holt, Hugh Farr, and Tim Spencer.

Don "Red" Barry, Republic's first new series star of the early forties.

9

DAREDEVILS
OF THE WEST

B-Westerns attained the pinnacle of their popularity in the early and middle forties. After that, rising costs and multiple other reasons forced the genre into attrition. As was the case in the preceding decade, we once again found some old favorites still prospering, some departing; some new faces survived, at least for a while, and others perished almost before they had left the starting gate in their race for success.

Republic Pictures Corporation was now the undisputed king of the B-Western producers, and at one time held down seven of the top ten positions in the *Motion Picture Herald* annual listing of the audience's Western favorites. Don "Red" Barry was the studio's first big new series star to make an appearance in the forties. Barry, small in size but large in talent and enthusiasm, had scored well as the lead in *Adventures of Red Ryder*, a serial produced by the studio in 1940, and a series all his own was inevitable. The Barry Westerns were a cut above the routine programmers fans had been used to. Instead of stressing just the action elements, Barry's scripts called for him to do a considerable amount of acting. Frequently his films would feature him in dual roles playing both a good guy and bad guy simultaneously. My favorite in the series, which consisted of twenty-nine films, was *The Tulsa Kid*, in which he came face to face with his outlaw foster father, beautifully played by Noah Beery, in the final showdown. During this series-making period Barry was loaned out to Twentieth Century-Fox

to do a role in *The Purple Heart*. Barry says that Darryl F. Zanuck was so impressed with him that he wanted to buy his contract from Republic, but Herbert Yates refused to sell and Barry's dreams of giant screen stardom at a major studio were dashed.

Another star who achieved major success with Republic was William Elliott. Over at Columbia Bill had become a big Western and serial favorite after having appeared in numerous villain and bit roles in the early and middle thirties. Republic now featured him with George "Gabby" Hayes and Anne Jeffreys in a series of eight action-packed adventures that began with *Calling Wild Bill Elliott* in 1943. In one of the films, *Wagon Tracks West*, one of his main adversaries was Tom Tyler, who played an Indian called Clawtooth. Elliott had several things going for him: first, he had an extremely infectious and winning personality; second, he looked good on screen because he was tall and lanky and did creditably well in the action sequences, although he was doubled frequently in those Republic years by Tom Steele; finally, he was an excellent horseman, and it was a sheer pleasure to watch him ride full tilt over those Republic exterior locations. After this series of eight films Elliott did sixteen Red Ryder features and then went into big budget productions.

Sunset Carson made only fifteen features and one guest-star appearance in Roy Rogers's *Bells of Rosarita*, but he was one of Republic's best-

145

received stars. The studio had started him out in films that top-billed Smiley Burnette like *Call of the Rockies* and *Bordertown Trail* in 1944, but Republic soon got rid of the comic, who off-screen was far from pleasant or amusing, and boosted Carson to the lead spot. It took some doing to make an actor out of the giant cowpoke. One story maintained that his delivery of lines was so bad (he ran them all together without pausing) that co-stars Tom London and Peggy Stewart actually painted a huge period on a piece of cardboard and told Carson to stop every time they held it up out of camera range and count to four before he delivered his next line. If you look closely you can see his lips moving slightly in some scenes as he did just that. But regardless of minor details like acting, Sunset was topnotch in the action category and that is really what counted with the fans. One of his films, *Santa Fe Saddlemates*, is the virtual model of an all-action B-Western. In the opening five minutes he has three fights (a test to determine his qualifications for handling a dangerous mission) and a reel or so later has another big brawl in a saloon. Finally, at the film's finale, he has a long chase followed by another humdinger of a battle with the film's villain, Roy Barcroft in a blacksmith shop. Films like *El Paso Kid*, *Sheriff of Cimarron*, *The Cherokee Flash*, and *Rio Grande Raiders* all had more than the usual share of thrills, and it was easy to see why claims were made that he was getting more fan mail from southern states than Rogers and Autry. In *Rio Grande Raiders*, incidentally, Sunset's brother was played by diminutive Bob Steele, who looked like a kid standing next to the giant star. Carson's career was finished at the studio after a succession of personal conflicts and a serious automobile accident.

In addition to these films, Republic was still riding high with its Three Mesquiteers, Roy Rogers, and Gene Autry features, but they did meet failure when they tried to star Eddie Dew in a series in which he was to play a character called John Paul Revere. Bob Livingston was brought in to take over the role after two films, but the series folded rapidly.

Over at Monogram Jack Randall, Tom Keene, and Tex Ritter were wrapping up their series with the company and a search for *new* faces found the studio turning up with *old* faces when they brought Buck Jones, Tim McCoy, and Raymond Hatton in to do the Rough Riders series,

and Ken Maynard, Hoot Gibson and Bob Steele in to do the Trail Blazers films. For good measure, they had the Range Busters as a watered-down version of the Three Mesquiteers. All three new series had thrown in the towel by 1944, and the studio signed Johnny Mack Brown, who had left Universal when that studio had decided to cut down on its B-Western output, and Raymond Hatton to star in a new series to replace the Rough Riders string of features that was broken when Buck Jones died. Brown and Hatton became the studio's bread-and-butter winners for almost ten solid years. The only other series at Monogram of any real merit was that which featured Gilbert Roland as the Cisco Kid. Roland had followed Cesar Romero, who had picked up the role after Warner Baxter had finished with it at Twentieth Century-Fox, and lent his own authentic Latin charm to the character in films like *South of Monterey* and *King of the Bandits* in 1946 and 1947.

Columbia Pictures had Bill Elliott, Tex Ritter, and Russell Hayden riding the range for them for a brief period in the early forties, but they soon departed and it was left mainly up to Charles Starrett to supply the thrills and excitement in a long string of Durango Kid vehicles until Gene Autry joined the studio in the late forties to give its Western schedule some diversity. Starrett was a pro all the way and handled a good many of his own stunts in the early days. However, as he grew older, and since he had the considerable advantage of often having his face covered by a black mask, young Jock Mahoney began to do most of the daredevil work, and it made it appear that the older Starrett became the more exciting he looked on the screen.

PRC had several lackluster series going for them featuring Bob Steele and Buster Crabbe as Billy the Kid, George Houston as the Lone Rider, and Dave O'Brien, James Newill and Guy Wilkerson as the Texas Rangers, but there was little that was good that could be said about them. Production values were almost nil and the musical background scores were so bad that most of us cringed when we heard them. Casting off his Billy the Kid tag, Crabbe did do some above-average work in a series which paired him with Al "Fuzzy" St. John, but his many fans surely must have wished that he could have made his films at another studio.

RKO continued to make good use of George O'Brien in an excellent series of features, but

Don "Red" Barry and his frequent co-star, lovely Lynn Merrick, in *Carson City Cyclone* (Republic 1943).

World War II interrupted him at his peak and when he returned from service his fine career was virtually finished. The studio had also started young Tim Holt on his road to stardom as a Western action star and lost him to service duty as well, but in Holt's case he was still young enough when he returned to pick up right where he left off, and he continued making Westerns until 1952.

Universal, deprived of Johnny Mack Brown, had to be content with the services of Rod Cameron, Eddie Dew, and Kirby Grant. Of the three, only Cameron really delivered the goods, and he quickly moved up the ladder to better quality features.

This period also saw isolated attempts to create new stars and series with varying degrees of success. Russell Hayden was excellent in a few Northwest Mounted Police adventures which had unusually short running times (about forty-five minutes) and were made in color. Twentieth Century-Fox put George Montgomery, who had done bit and stunt duty at Republic for several years, into new remakes of Zane Grey features like *Last of the Duanes* and *Riders of the Purple Sage*, but he quickly moved up to become a handsome leading man in the studio's

big-budget productions. The same studio also introduced a newcomer called John Kimbrough, but he was a complete failure. Republic, in addition to missing the mark with Eddie Dew, also came a cropper with Ray Middleton when they tried to build him into a new star in *Hurricane Smith*. Robert Mitchum had spent years playing bad guys in Hopalong Cassidy and Johnny Mack Brown adventures. Finally RKO tried to give him a break and featured him in the Zane Grey story *Nevada*, with Richard Martin as his sidekick. Instant stardom beckoned, though, when he was cast in *The Story of G.I. Joe*, and his B-Western career was left in the lurch.

All things considered, we were lucky indeed to have had this particular period in screen history to enjoy week after week as children. The B-Western had matured from those early days of awkward realism and was now a slickly produced commodity that fulfilled almost all our childhood demands. Perhaps there wasn't as much location work as one might have wished, but there was action in generous portions, and that was all that we Western fans asked for.

Noah Beery and Don "Red" Barry in *The Tulsa Kid* (Republic 1940), one of the best in the series of twenty-nine Republic Barry B-Westerns.

Don "Red" Barry was once married to popular Republic leading lady Peggy Stewart. This photograph of the couple was taken in 1942.

"Wild Bill" Elliott reaches for one of his famous reversible guns, to the consternation of Slim Whittaker, in *Hands Across the Rockies* (Columbia 1941).

"Wild Bill" Elliott and George "Gabby" Hayes search out some more action in the Republic cave sets in *The Man from Thunder River* (Republic 1943).

"Wild Bill" Elliott shows an important clue to George "Gabby" Hayes while Harry Woods, playing a good guy for a change, looks on in *Bordertown Gunfighters* (Republic 1943).

Sunset Carson was a popular series star at Republic. This scene is from one of his best films, *The Cherokee Flash* (Republic 1945).

Sunset Carson helps foil a robbery attempt for the benefit of Jack Kirk and Linda Stirling in *Sheriff of Cimarron* (Republic 1945).

Linda Stirling and Sunset Carson in *Santa Fe Saddlemates* (Republic 1945).

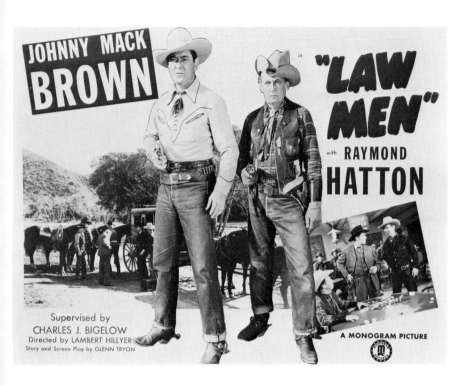

Johnny Mack Brown assists a wounded Kenneth MacDonald while pal Raymond Hatton looks on in *West of the Rio Grande* (Monogram 1944).

Charles King gets the drop on Jack Randall while bareheaded George Chesebro takes our hero's gun in *Wild Horse Range* (Monogram 1940).

George "Gabby" Hayes, my favorite sidekick. Gabby was a regular with William Boyd, William Elliott, and Roy Rogers in many of their series' features.

A rare publicity shot of Gene Autry and Jack Randall taken in the early forties.

Jack Kirk, Allan Lane, Kenne Duncan, and Tom London in *Trail of Kit Carson* (Republic 1945), one of a series of six films Lane made before taking over the Red Ryder character in 1946.

Smiley Burnette was a popular sidekick for Gene Autry and Charles Starrett, as well as a star in a few features on his own.

Fuzzy Knight was Universal's big comic sidekick, appearing with almost all of that studio's stars at one time or another, particularly with Johnny Mack Brown.

Russell Hayden and Charles Starrett in *Overland to Deadwood* (Columbia 1942).

Frank Hagney, *left*, keeps a gun on Buster Crabbe while Kermit Maynard holds his arm in *Blazing Frontier* (PRC 1941).

Dick Curtis was Charles Starrett's most frequent adversary. Here they appear in a scene from *Cowboy in the Clouds* (Columbia 1943).

Chris Pin Martin as Pancho, *left*, and Cesar Romero as the Cisco Kid in *Romance of the Rio Grande* (Twentieth Century-Fox 1941). Romero had taken the role over from Warner Baxter, who had played the character earlier for the same studio.

Gilbert Roland, *left*, was the third Cisco Kid when the series moved to Monogram. In *King of the Bandits* (Monogram 1947) Chris Pin Martin again played his pal, Pancho.

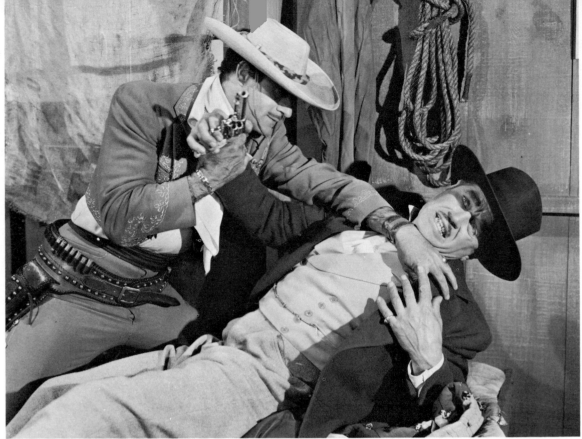

Gilbert Roland, as the Cisco Kid, battled veteran badman Harry Woods in *South of Monterey* (Monogram 1946).

Lee " 'lasses" White looks like he's been in trouble again. Tim Holt, *center*, and Ray Whitley, *right*, join in the fun in *Thundering Hoofs* (RKO 1941).

Helen Talbot was another favorite leading lady in Republic B-Westerns, making many with, among others, Don "Red" Barry and Allan Lane. In this production shot from the serial *King of the Forest Rangers* (Republic 1946) she poses with visiting director Frank Borzage, ace cameraman Bud Thackery, in white shirt, and famed action director Spencer Gordon Bennet.

Linda Stirling, one of Republic's—and audiences—favorite leading ladies in B-Westerns.

Columbia's claim to the B-Western queen title was Iris Meredith.

Ray Whitley, Eddie Dew, and Rod Cameron in *Riders of the Santa Fe* (Universal 1944).

Smiley Burnette and Bob Livingston in *Pride of the Plains* (Republic 1943), one of a short series of features which had begun with Eddie Dew as the star in which the studio had hoped to introduce a character called John Paul Revere. Even with Livingston playing the role, it just didn't catch on.

Neath Canadian Skies (Screen Guild 1948) starring Russell Hayden, *left*, was one of many independent action films made during the period. That's Kermit Maynard with the rifle.

Republic tried to build Ray Middleton into a Western star in *Hurricane Smith* (Republic 1941) with dismal results.

George Montgomery, *left*, assists Francis Ford, famous director John Ford's brother, in *Last of the Duanes* (Twentieth Century-Fox 1941), one of a new series of remakes of Zane Grey stories.

RKO tried to build Robert Mitchum into a series Western star, but he went on to greater fame as a leading man before the series really got rolling. In *Nevada* (RKO 1944) Richard Martin was his guitar-strumming sidekick. Martin went on to become Tim Holt's pal in Holt's long string of popular RKO Westerns.

John Kimbrough, *right*, was another big failure as a series star. Here, in *Lone Star Ranger* (Twentieth Century-Fox 1942), he appears with Truman Bradley, *left*, and Jonathan Hale.

An interesting one-shot was *Silver Stallion* (Monogram 1941) with Chief Thunder-cloud, LeRoy Mason, and stunt ace David Sharpe.

A big failure at Republic was Eddie Dew, *right*, in two starring features. In this scene from *Raiders of Sunset Pass* (Republic 1943) he has Roy Barcroft covered.

Elliott and Peggy Stewart in *Conquest of Cheyenne* (Republic 1946). This was Bill's final appearance as Red Ryder.

10
TWENTY-THREE
HOURS OF THRILLS

Every B-Western fan had his own particular favorite star or series whom he enjoyed more than any other during his young moviegoing days. For those who grew up in the twenties it might have been Jack Holt or Tom Mix or some other silent saddle ace; for thirties fans, perhaps Bob Steele, Ken Maynard, Tom Tyler, or Tim McCoy was their particular dish of oats. My moviegoing period, the early and middle forties, had numerous choices available to whet any action fan's appetite, including Gene Autry, Roy Rogers, Sunset Carson, Charles Starrett. But I found myself enjoying most the series of twenty-three features made by Republic between 1944 and 1947 based on the exploits of the famous comic-strip hero, Red Ryder. These films were the answer to an action-lover's prayer. Filmed during those glorious days at Republic when the stunt team was at its slam-bang, set-destroying peak, almost every one of the twenty-three films was loaded to the brim with exciting chases, fights, and assorted action highlights.

Republic had brought the Red Ryder character to the screen four years earlier in serial form. Donald Barry had scored a personal triumph in the John Wayne film *Wyoming Outlaw* and studio head Herbert J. Yates decided to give Barry the leading role in what was sure to be an action-packed adventure classic. Right from the start Barry rebelled against his casting. He felt he didn't resemble the character at all physically, and he did not want to work in serials, which he felt were demeaning as they were aimed at a primarily juvenile audience. Yates convinced him to take the role, and Barry reluctantly turned in a performance that made him a star and tagged him with the Don "Red" Barry screen name, which he also hated because he really didn't have red hair. The serial did, indeed, turn out to be a huge success, due in no small part to the excellent action work turned in by stuntman David Sharpe, who doubled Barry in most of the really exciting moments of the twelve-chapter delight. The complete serial was filmed in less than a month. It had a simple plot which found villain Harry Worth out to grab valuable property which he intended to sell to a railroad for a right of way at his own price. When the serial was completed, Barry went into his own series of action features, and the Red Ryder character remained dormant until Republic could find someone new who would be able to handle the role successfully.

That chance came in 1944 in the person of William "Wild Bill" Elliott. Elliott had had a successful career for several years at Columbia where he made Westerns and serials that pleased most fans. Republic acquired his services and starred him with George "Gabby" Hayes in a series of eight exciting Western features in 1943 and 1944. Elliott was strictly playing himself, with all the gimmicks he had used at Columbia still very much in evidence, including his favorite tag line, "I'm a peaceable man, but . . ." which usually prefaced a slam-bang fight sequence. Republic decided that Elliott would do the Red Ryder character justice and immediately had him do eight features which were released between May, 1944, and May, 1945. There are those who argue, and quite justifiably, that Elliott was not really playing Fred Harman's character but only himself, and that he completely changed the comic-strip image to reflect his own image (the reversible guns, the stylized shirt, etc.). The charge is quite true, but so what? As fans who looked only for action we really didn't care about the character's name or source as long as he delivered the necessary thrills and excitement, and Elliott *did* supply just what we wanted. So while the purists cried "fraud" and grumbled, many millions just enjoyed.

The series began with two films in which George "Gabby" Hayes was still Elliott's partner, *Tucson Raiders* and *Marshal of Reno*. The former found Red and friends trying to thwart the tyranny of a villainous Governor (Stanley Andrews) and had a rousing finale in which the villains were blown up, courtesy of special-effects artist Howard Lydecker, who created a spectacular miniature for a tremendous barn explosion. In the latter Red proves the innocence of a young man who was framed for murder. The young man, incidentally, was played by Blake Edwards, who went on to become a famous producer-director. *The San Antonio Kid*, a routine effort to be sure, followed but then came *Cheyenne Wildcat*, my favorite of the sixteen Elliott Ryders. In this film Red opposed the supreme villainy of Roy Barcroft, who went around murdering his victims with thrown knives. The film had four great fight sequences, and Barcroft was dispatched in memorable fashion. During the finale, Red and Roy stage a massive brawl during which the latter throws a knife that misses Red and goes through a door panel, leaving the blade exposed. Naturally, at the end of the fight Roy is knocked against the door and killed by his own weapon. I can still see Barcroft standing silently against the door as Red wonders why his opponent has suddenly stopped throwing punches and is just staring open-eyed. Another crowd-pleaser followed immediately with the title *Vigilantes of Dodge City*, in which Red did battle with Le-Roy Mason and Hal Taliaferro, who were out to try and gain the Duchess's freight line. The Duchess was played by that fine character actress Alice Fleming in all sixteen of the Elliott films, and Ryder's constant sidekick, Little

Beaver, was played in all twenty-three features by Bobby Blake, who matured into an excellent actor in later years in such films as *The Purple Gang, In Cold Blood* and *Tell Them Willie Boy Is Here*. The remaining titles in the first series, *Sheriff of Las Vegas, The Great Stagecoach Robbery,* and *Lone Texas Ranger,* were milder in overall thrills, but were still big enough at the box-office to warrant the studio's making a second series of eight titles, which were released between August, 1945, and April, 1946. This second set began with *Phantom of the Plains* (which contained a spectacular fight sequence and stagecoach chase that ran for almost the entire last two reels of the film and which is hard to beat for sheer continued action) and continued with *Marshal of Laredo, Colorado Pioneers* (which featured a trouble-prone collection of scene-stealing kids), *Wagon Wheels Westward* (which had Roy Barcroft riding into a mysteriously deserted town and taking it over in order to swindle Red and a bunch of new homesteaders who were traveling there to settle down), *California Gold Rush* (which really had nothing to do with California *or* a gold rush), *Sheriff of Redwood Valley* (in which former cowboy great Bob Steele had a meaty role as a former crook who was trying to go straight), *Sun Valley Cyclone* (which purported to tell the story of how Red first acquired his famous horse, Thunder) and, finally, *Conquest of Cheyenne,* which had Peggy Stewart riding around in a newfangled horseless carriage and causing Red all kinds of trouble in one of the weakest films in the entire series.

After sixteen films Elliott had had enough of Red Ryder. He wanted better roles, and the studio obliged him by giving him big productions which may have flattered his ego but which cost him his legion of devoted Saturday afternoon fans.

The studio began auditioning new actors to fill the Ryder vacancy, including young Marshall Reed who had played numerous minor roles and did stunt work at Republic, and was featured in Johnny Mack Brown vehicles at Monogram. He might have gotten the part if Herbert Yates hadn't seen a clip from one of the six Westerns Allan Lane had turned out in 1944 and 1945. He is said to have remarked at a private screening, pointing at the screen where Lane was on view, "That's my new Red Ryder!"

For a great many people, Lane was a better physical choice to play the character of Red

Ryder. It really boils down to a matter of personal choice. I enjoyed Elliott and Lane almost equally. The first film in the series, *Santa Fe Uprising*, was released in September, 1946, and was an action-packed debut in which Lane matched wits with class-A badman Barton Mac-Lane, who was out to control a toll road owned by the Duchess, now played in these final seven features by Martha Wentworth. The finale featured a great shoot-out and fight in the famous Republic cave sets, which were located on the studio lot adjacent to the famous blacksmith shop set where so many outstanding fight sequences were staged. *Stagecoach to Denver* followed and was one of the weaker Lane entries, but the following feature, *Vigilantes of Boomtown*, had a most unusual and entertaining plot. "Gentleman" Jim Corbett (George Turner) and Bob Fitzsimmons (John Dehner) arrive in Carson City to train for their world heavyweight bout. Peggy Stewart tries to get them to leave the territory because she feels boxing is brutal and she feels people will consider the townspeople savages for tolerating the planned slugfest. Into this situation rides evil Roy Barcroft, who intends to rob the proceeds from the planned spectacle, but who is finally thwarted by Red. He fights Roy with professional boxing punches taught to him by none other than Jim Corbett. The whole thing was a lot of fun and well worth viewing. *Homesteaders of Paradise Valley* and *Oregon Trail Scouts*, two routine but entertaining features, followed. Then came *Marshal of Cripple Creek*, which is very likely the best of the Lane Ryders, and one of the best B-Westerns Republic ever turned out. The cast was loaded with pros like Trevor Bardette, Tom London, and Roy Barcroft. Bardette comes to Cripple Creek with his family in the hopes of making a fast fortune. He falls in with Gene Stutenroth, who tricks him into hijacking an ore wagon. Bardette is caught and goes to jail. In the meantime, his son arrives in town and very quickly falls under Stutenroth's influence. Red tells the bandit leader to leave the kid alone or "I'll break you

in two." Meanwhile, Barcroft winds up in prison in a cell next to Bardette and tells the latter that Red is making things tough for his son. "Why," Roy says, "he's even got him cleaning out *spittoons*." Well, that would be enough to make any man break out of jail, and Bardette does. The film ends on a frantic note with Bardette convinced that Ryder is right, and he dies saving Red's life. Ryder, in turn, goes to Stutenroth's saloon where, after telling him, "I told you if you didn't leave that kid alone I'd break you in two," proceeds to do just that in a terrific slugfest. This was entertainment to be sure, at its supercharged best. The final film in the series, *Rustlers of Devil's Canyon*, found Red combating an evil Arthur Space who was supposedly the friendly town doctor, but who was in reality the head of a gang of rustlers. With the conclusion of this final Ryder feature Lane tacked on his nickname of "Rocky" and did a long and successful series for Republic that continued into the fifties.

Republic no longer utilized the Ryder character, but Eagle-Lion turned out four features starring Jim Bannon as Red in 1949. Filmed in color, *Ride, Ryder, Ride; Roll, Thunder, Roll; The Fighting Redhead;* and *The Cowboy and the Prize Fighter* were generally awful, but Bannon, for those good old purists, did look quite a bit as you would expect a real-life Red Ryder to look.

Informed sources say that a television pilot was made with Allan Lane playing Red again, but it was never sold and I have been unable to verify the information.

All in all, those twenty-three features produced by Republic satisfied completely my enormous Saturday afternoon craving for thrills, and my memories of those films are still vivid even today. From the very first entrance of the characters (remember Red and Little Beaver walking out of a giant-sized replica of a Red Ryder book?) in the opening credits, to the final fade-out, it was polished Republic professionalism all the way—and what more could any Western fan really ask for?

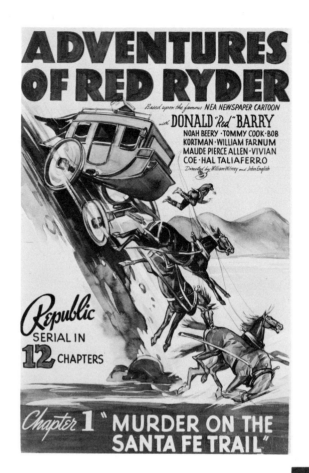

William "Wild Bill" Elliott as comic-strip hero Red Ryder, one of his most popular characterizations.

Don "Red" Barry comes to the aid of Hal Talia-ferro as villainous Harry Worth looks on in *Adventures of Red Ryder* (Republic 1940), the only serial to feature the Red Ryder character.

Don "Red" Barry, hairpiece and all, and Tommy Cook, as Little Beaver, in *Adventures of Red Ryder* (Republic 1940).

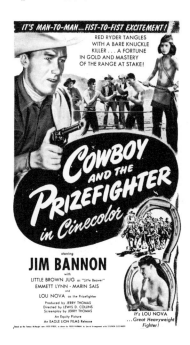

Alice Fleming was the Duchess in the sixteen Elliott Red Ryder films, and Bobby Blake played Little Beaver in all twenty-three features. This portrait was from *Marshal of Reno* (Republic 1944).

Phantom of the Plains (Republic 1945) had a finale which found Elliott battling William Haade, playing Ace Hanlon, and Ian Keith, *right*, on top of a runaway stagecoach.

Elliott gets the drop on Don Costello in *Marshal of Laredo* (Republic 1945). In the film Costello's face had been disfigured by fire, and his villainous boss, Roy Barcroft, kept flipping lighted matches at him whenever he didn't obey orders quickly enough.

William Haade, *left*, Bud Geary, and Kenne Duncan think they are going to give Elliott a good going-over in *Sheriff of Las Vegas* (Republic 1944), but I somehow feel they will be sadly disappointed.

In *Sheriff of Redwood Valley* (Republic 1946) cowboy star Bob Steele played a former bad guy now going straight. Peggy Stewart and John Wayne Wright (I wonder who he was named after?) played Bob's wife and son.

Roy Barcroft wants Elliott to get the point in
Cheyenne Wildcat (Republic 1944).

Elliott battles veteran stuntman-actor Fred Graham
in *Great Stagecoach Robbery* (Republic 1945).

A rare shot of the two Red Ryders together attending the opening of the Hitching Post Theatre in Beverly Hills. Lane was playing Red on the screen at the time.

Elliott catches up to master villain Dick Curtis in *Wagon Wheels Westward* (Republic 1945).

A new family portrait of the Ryder clan, with Allan Lane as Red, Bobby Blake as Little Beaver, and Martha Wentworth as the Duchess, from *Santa Fe Uprising* (Republic 1946).

Arthur Space, *right*, who is really the film's villain, ties up Pierce Lyden while Allan Lane supervises in *Rustlers of Devil's Canyon* (Republic 1947).

Allan Lane as Fred Harman's famous comic-strip hero, Red Ryder.

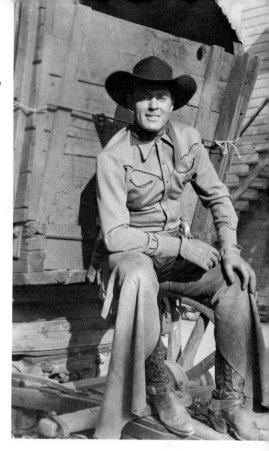

George Turner, *left*, shakes hands with John Dehner as Bobby Blake, Roscoe Karns, and Martha Wentworth look on with Allan Lane in *Vigilantes of Boomtown* (Republic 1947).

Allan Lane gives Dick Curtis back his gun after knocking him all over the place in *Santa Fe Uprising* (Republic 1946).

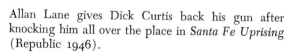

Allan Lane promised Gene Stutenroth early in *Marshal of Cripple Creek* (Republic 1947) that he would "break him in two" if he didn't quit his villainy. At the film's finale, Lane almost kept his word completely in a terrific battle sequence.

Allan Lane gives Roy Barcroft some friendly advice, which Roy will naturally decline to follow, in *Marshal of Cripple Creek* (Republic 1947).

Jim Bannon, *center*, made a good-looking Red Ryder in a series of four color films in 1949, but overall the features left fans cold. Emmett Lynn, *right*, was Bannon's sidekick in this scene from *The Fighting Redhead* (Eagle-Lion 1949).

Allan "Rocky" Lane was one of Republic's last big
series stars, continuing to make Westerns of varying
quality until the studio ceased production in 1953.

11
THE END
OF THE TRAIL

As the forties drew to a close, the B-Western well found itself running dry. Too many external forces were being brought in to combat the continuance of the little action gems most of us had grown up with. Costs over the years had risen spectacularly. In the thirties an hour-long film could be brought in for well under the fifty-thousand-dollar mark; now the same film would cost over a hundred thousand, and with no appreciable upgrading of quality. Also, many of the smaller theaters were folding their screens thanks to the continuing dollar squeeze, thus limiting audience attendance to an unprofitable level. An even greater element of concern to film producers was the looming specter of television, which was even then beginning to make itself felt. But the saddest of all these detrimental forces was the complete lack of vision on the studios' part in developing any really interesting new personalities to replace those who, for one reason or another, were beginning to lose their box-office appeal; while at the same time major studios were introducing a variety of screen newcomers in color presentations that were far more satisfying to general audiences.

It was Republic, as usual, who best weathered the storm until the inevitable finale. Herbert J. Yates, the head of Republic, couldn't have cared less about the Western product the studio was turning out. His big interest was in producing big color films featuring his wife, Vera Hruba Ralston. Not only were many of these films bad, but the drain of money from the studio's coffers

to produce them almost completely wiped out the company. Minority stockholders brought suit against Yates, and in one case they even forced Ralston's name to be removed from its usual place of prominence in theatrical posters and advertising. The slow deterioration of Republic over the years was not pleasant for loyal fans to watch. In the thirties the company spared no expense to shoot their low-budget films outdoors in attractive locations with a minimum of indoor studio work. Gradually, however, for reasons of convenience and economy, more and more footage was actually shot on the studio's sound stages. Now instead of long exterior chases we would see stock footage mixed with gross interior close-ups against a rear projection screen. We were exposed to a veritable plethora of fake trees, fake rocks, fake buildings. The only thing that seemed real were the players, and we sometimes had our doubts about them, too. But it wasn't a complete loss in those declining years. In all fairness it should be admitted that Republic did make a reasonable effort to try and maintain its superiority in the field it had so admirably dominated for over a decade.

Gene Autry, who had in fact put Republic on the map in the thirties, returned after World War II to find his cinema rival Roy Rogers at the top of the Western ladder, and after one short series at his alma mater he decided, for monetary and creative reasons, to transfer his allegiance to Columbia. There, under his own producing arm, he turned in some interesting and popular work until the early fifties. Rogers, on the other hand, was going through another stage in his cycle of development. He had started in a series of frontier-type period pieces, then moved into the big musical-Western production-plus category. Now he experimented with the studio's Trucolor process and somewhat more adult story lines. As an actor he had matured extremely well. He looked good, acted capably, and was an excellent horseman. Under the stimulus of fine writers and directors, Rogers inevitably gave an entertaining afternoon to his fans in film after film until he, too, left to enter television production in the early fifties.

Allan "Rocky" Lane, who had built his reputation on fast-moving serial and Western work, began his third series of familiar action pieces in 1947. The first few films were generally excellent, but the series quickly fell into the pattern of using too much stock and too little ingenuity. In most of these films he was usually opposing the villainy of Roy Barcroft, who gave a considerable boost to the overall quality of the product. Still, with all their obvious faults, the series met with commercial success, and Lane was voted into the Top Ten Western Stars listing several times.

Republic did try to bring in new faces but met little success in building them to the prominence achieved by men like Bill Elliott, Don "Red" Barry, and others. Monte Hale had played bit parts for years at the studio and was finally given a chance at stardom in a series that started out with the help of Trucolor. He just couldn't make the grade and was dropped after a few short years. However, the series did offer the frequent casting of Adrian Booth (formerly Lorna Gray) as Monte's leading lady, and that did give us some solace. Rex Allen started his career in a film called *The Arizona Cowboy,* and he quickly adopted the title as a nickname. He was a pleasant enough performer, and the studio, again, tried to give him enough good films to build him into a major star. He did achieve some success, but primarily because there was so little competition. As one of the last of the singing cowboys, he reigned until Republic closed its doors, and the lanky redhead eventually went into the lucrative field of off-screen narration, where he did many films for Walt Disney, both theatrical and television, and a long series of commercials for Purina Dog Chow. Speaking of off-screen narration, even

Rex's frequent screen adversary, Roy Barcroft, did the narration for several Disney television shows in the sixties, as well as starring in the Spin and Marty series for the Mickey Mouse Club show. As an experiment, Republic even tried to do a Western series featuring a young boy, Michael Chapin, as the star, but that series met with almost instant failure and was quickly dropped.

Over at Monogram Westerns were in even more dismal straits. Johnny Mack Brown, who had stepped in after the studio's earlier Rough Riders series had folded with the death of Buck Jones, was really beginning to show his age. He had put on considerable weight, and the scripts they were giving him to work with now were slow-moving and unentertaining. It was a shame, for Johnny had been popular since the early thirties and was one of the more convincing cowboy stars. After doing more than sixty films in the series, Johnny rode into the retirement sunset.

Monogram tried to foist two new personalities on us in those days, and the results were not good even though both actors made numerous films. Jimmy Wakely had been around in films for years with his trio doing song-fillers in the Westerns of other stars like Johnny Mack Brown and Don "Red" Barry. As a singing cowboy he was not up to par with Autry and Rogers, or even Rex Allen for that matter, and as an action hero he fell into an even lower category. Another real dud, although he did have an amazing legion of loyal fans who admired him for many of the same reasons Sunset Carson's fans had admired him, was Whip Wilson. Whip delivered lines as though he didn't know what they meant, and his whip seemed to have a great deal more personality than he had.

There were a few last-ditch Monogram stars who were able to last into the fifties, however, and who were still able to deliver convincing work. Duncan Renaldo had inherited the Cisco Kid series from Gilbert Roland and did a good job whenever the scripts would let him. Kirby Grant, who had made some films for Universal in the early forties, did a series of Northwest Mounted Police films with Chinook the Wonder Dog getting co-star billing. They were good actioners and, at least, offered some varied location work. William Elliott, who had scored immense success at Republic, now found himself doing features for Monogram (who had changed their corporate name to Allied Artists) that were an attempt to revive the action format of earlier years. The stories were generally above average, and Elliott, as always, gave very satisfactory performances. Unfortunately, Elliott wound up his screen career in a series of non-Western crime mellers instead of tall in the saddle. The studio wrapped up its B-Western production with an abysmal series of films starring Wayne Morris. Morris had enjoyed some degree of popularity in the thirties but, after returning from World War II service, found the going rough. He was most unconvincing, and nobody cared much to have a cowboy hero with a protruding beer-belly as a screen idol.

Columbia's primary contribution to the Western field was the continuing adventures of that masked avenger, the Durango Kid, played by Charles Starrett, and a few musicals with outdoor backgrounds. Starrett, who kept in excellent shape, was still effective even though the action chores were increasingly being turned over to Jock Mahoney. RKO was still turning out fine Tim Holt entries that were filmed in interesting locations and had some excellent action sequences. At the same time, other studios and independent companies turned out some real losers. Sunset Carson, having left Republic, starred in a terrible series of features that were shot in 16mm and blown up to 35mm for theaters. The stories were awful, the filming was awful, the sound was awful, and he was awful. It was a pity, for Carson had turned out some fine work at Republic when under the direction of capable hands. PRC gave us two heroes in the persons of "Lash" LaRue and Eddie Dean. LaRue talked and behaved like a very poor imitation of Humphrey Bogart. Unfortunately, he couldn't *act* like Bogart, and, like Whip Wilson, the best thing about him was his handling of the whip. Fortunately, Al "Fuzzy" St. John was along to at least give the films a few laughs. Eddie Dean had played bit parts in so many films that I am sure he lost any hope of ever achieving stardom. Usually playing badmen, he popped up in the films of Boyd, Autry, Rogers, Barry, and others with amazing frequency. When he finally did get his big chance in a series with some films made in color, the results were often uneven. When he had good character-actor support and a good script, he was tolerable, and one could even take pleasure

in his singing, which was a cut above average. But when the elements of good film construction were against him, well, the less said the better. RKO tried to build James Warren into a new hero, but failed completely after only a few films.

But the shoddiest attempt to shortchange audiences was in a series of films made by two former "Lucky" portrayers in the Hopalong Cassidy films, James Ellison and Russell Hayden. Both extremely capable performers under the direction of others, they banded together and produced six films all at the same time. Utilizing one set of excellent character actors, they simply shifted them around from one film to the next with each playing a different, or sometimes the same, role. No change of costumes, no change of scenery, no solid story quality, no professional polish, no anything! While television production was soon to be similarly geared to quick production, Saturday afternoon crowds were not yet ready for this ludicrous attempt at a cinematic swindle. The chicanery was even carried over to television, where the very same films were retitled for no really apparent reason.

For a time the B-Western was a staple of early television. Fans could turn on the set and see at least two or three of their cowboy favorites each day. However, television soon began to make its own half-hour and hour-long shows, and so there was no longer any need to pay large sums of money to rent earlier, and often quite poorly produced, Western fare. Add to the question of finances the persistent appeal by parents that these early films were much too violent, with excessive and gratuitous killing, and it was only a matter of time before stations would bow to the pressure and, with rare exceptions, pull them completely off the air. On occasion you might see them pop up on a southern station or on some UHF channel (primarily because with a limited market they can be obtained very cheaply), but generally the now-aging Western fan must sit back and be content with his memories of hundreds of thrilling afternoons spent watching those favorite saddle aces mete out their own particular brand of justice. Will we ever see their like again?

Monte Hale throws a realistic punch to stuntman Fred Graham in *Son of God's Country* (Republic 1948).

Monte Hale and his frequent leading lady in his Republic films, Adrian Booth (called Lorna Gray in her earlier screen days).

Allan "Rocky" Lane in an apparently acrobatic fight sequence from *Salt Lake Raiders* (Republic 1950).

Monte Hale adds his name to those of other Republic stars in one of the studio's sidewalks. Watching are Tom London, *center*, young Bobby Blake, and Adrian Booth, who were working with him in *Out California Way* (Republic 1946).

Allan "Rocky" Lane met Clayton (Lone Ranger)
Moore and Gail (Annie Oakley) Davis in *Frontier
Investigator* (Republic 1949).

Johnny Mack Brown, showing signs of wear, keeps
apart two former Hopalong Cassidy sidekicks, Jimmy
Ellison, *left*, and Rand Brooks in *Man from the
Black Hills* (Monogram 1952).

Young Michael Chapin was one of the child stars of a brief series for Republic. Here he appears in a scene with veteran badman William Haade in *Buckaroo Sheriff of Texas* (Republic 1950).

Leo Carrillo and Duncan Renaldo as the screen's final Pancho and the Cisco Kid in *The Daring Caballero* (United Artists 1949).

Jimmy Wakely in *West of the Alamo* (Monogram 1946).

A murderous Tom Tyler, *right*, threatens young Tim Holt in *Rio Grande Patrol* (RKO 1950). Tyler was already beginning to show signs of the illness which was to shortly end his career, and his life, prematurely.

Kenne Duncan and Jimmy Wakely in *Gun Runner*
(Monogram 1949).

Charles Starrett as the masked Durango Kid faces
up to former Dead End Kid, William Halop, in
Challenge of the Range (Columbia 1949).

Whip Wilson, *left*, gets a little rough with Marshall
Reed in *Night Raiders* (Monogram 1952).

Whip Wilson engages in a little playfulness with
George Chesebro in *Gunslingers* (Monogram 1950).

Rex Allen, the Arizona Cowboy, Republic's last popular series star. In this publicity still he's all dressed up for duty in *Shadows of Tombstone* (Republic 1953).

Eddie Dean, *left*, and stuntman David Sharpe, playing an important leading role this time, in *Colorado Serenade* (PRC 1946).

Rex Allen throws a pretty convincing punch to the chin of stuntman Dale Van Sickel in *Thunder in God's Country* (Republic 1951).

A few years after his starring series at Republic, Monte Hale, *left*, wound up playing villains in films like *Yukon Vengeance* (Allied Artists 1954) opposite star Kirby Grant.

"Lash" LaRue, in black, and Al "Fuzzy" St. John seem to have poor John Merton at a slight disadvantage in *Cheyenne Takes Over* (PRC 1947).

A little bigger budget was spent on *The Return of Wildfire* (Screen Guild 1948) with Richard Arlen and, *right*, Reed Hadley, but even the fact that it was in "Glowing Sepia-Tone" didn't keep it from being just a small independent B-Western with a little extra polish added.

James Warren, here in *Code of the West* (RKO 1946) with Raymond Burr, *left*, and Carol Forman, was given a buildup as a new Western series star, but he lasted for only a few films.

Russell Hayden and James Ellison shortchanged the public by turning out a whole series of films made at the same time with the same cast members being shuffled around to play different roles in each new film. The results were awful, and even Hayden and Ellison look bored in this scene from *Fast on the Draw* (Lippert 1950).

Roy Rogers was still going strong right up until the early fifties. Here he gets the drop on stuntman Fred Graham while Penny Edwards watches in *Heart of the Rockies* (Republic 1951).

Gene Autry gets ready to shoot a riding sequence for one of his later films, *Hills of Utah* (Columbia 1951).

William Elliott wound up his series career doing items like *The Homesteaders* (Allied Artists 1953). In this scene from the film he appears with Ray Walker, *left*, and Robert Lowery.

Pudgy Wayne Morris holds the dubious distinction of being the star of the final series of B-Westerns turned out by the minor studios. Here in *The Marksman* (Allied Artists 1953) he appears with I. Stanford Jolley.